Making Soap From Scratch

How to Make Handmade Soap – A Beginners Guide and Beyond

Gregory Lee White

PREFACE

Don't fret too much over your first batch of soap. When I first began making soap, I dressed up like a crazed astronaut (petrified I'd burn myself with lye), and stood at the stove for hours stirring with a wooden spoon. Nonetheless, the final product was indeed soap. It barely had any lather, took forever to harden, and didn't feel that great on the skin. The batch turned rancid long before I ever thought about trying to use it all. In fact, I was so disappointed with my creation that it was another five months before I attempted to make soap again.

But, my hands have to be busy working on something. I suppose most of my particular talents when it comes to mixing up concoctions come from my paternal grandfather. Known to all his friends as "W.T.", he wanted the recipe he used in the kitchen to be his own. Simply cooking a meal wasn't enough for him. He developed a secret, family barbecue sauce that had diners lining up at family reunions, holidays, and American Legion picnics. His passion for making wine was so fanatical that he eventually dug his own wine cellar. The backyard had rows of plum trees as well as a grape arbor to fuel his hobby. He was always looking for a challenge, creating original tastes such as blackberry liqueur and rose-petal wine. I think of him every time I create a new soap recipe.

My own interest in body care products came when I worked as the assistant manager for the well-known skin care company, Garden Botanika. Around the same time, I saw the Sandra Bullock movie, *Practical Magic* (based on the book by Alice Hoffman), and fell in love with the look and feel of her little bath and botanical shop. When Garden Botanika down-sized and closed their locations in the Southern states, the interest in skincare stayed with me. Research took me down a slightly different path as I learned more and more about natural skincare versus the mass-produced selections found in so many stores today. So the urge hit me again and I decided to reread the books I had purchased about soap making to figure out where I had gone wrong. That was back in 1999. Today, our soap company, aromagregory.com, produces thousands of pounds of soap each year, all made using original recipes that either my partner or I created.

This is the journey I will take you on - the beginning process of making good soap that is great for your skin. Once you get started and get the hang of it, beware. With so many scents and ingredients to choose from, it can become an addiction. The guest room may become the soap factory. Your friends will wish you would just stop talking about soap! The ledge of our bath tub looks like a cemetery where rows and rows of soap line up side by side, waiting to see which one will strike our fancy for a quick morning shower or a relaxing bath at night.

In the first part of the book, I will explain how to make soap the regular way, by pulling out your ingredients, weighing and melting your oils, etc. (we'll get to exactly how in a bit). This method is a good way of making small batches of soap just for friends and family. Also, the recipes include a wider variety of ingredients and let you experiment with different carrier oils.

The second part of the book focuses on what is called master-batch soap making. This is when you premix all of your carrier oils (olive, coconut, canola, etc.) and let them sit at room temperature until it is time to make soap. This method is good for making a lot of soap in a short amount of time and will focus on recipes that include just a few good carrier oils.

Are you ready to begin? There is no turning back once you get the feel for this creative and rewarding form of art.

G.L.W.

OTHER BOOKS BY GREGORY LEE WHITE

CLUCKED – The Tale of Pickin Chicken

ESSENTIAL OILS AND AROMATHERAPY: How to Use Essential Oils for
Beauty, Health, and Spirituality

LITTLE HOUSE SEARCH: A Puzzle Book and Tour of the Works of Laura
Ingalls Wilder

CONTENTS

Author's Note

The first edition of MAKING SOAP FROM SCRATCH focused primarily on the way that I make soap – in larger quantities. Based on reader response, this second edition has added more recipes to the standard method of making soap. In addition, I have included techniques such as swirling colors, how to cut soap, curing soap, and how to calculate soap mold volume. Also, there is information on labeling and packaging soap, how to sell it, and how to set up a craft fair booth. I thank all of the readers for their feedback about what they would like to see in the second edition.

ACKNOWLEDGMENTS

For my partner, Roy, who encourages my writing and everything else I do. My thanks to Cathy for editing my rambling voice into clean instructions.

ALL ABOUT SOAP

You'll be surprised to learn that many of the ingredients that go into soap making are already in your kitchen. Soap is the end result of mixing oils, lye, and water. Whether you pull it off the supermarket shelf, buy the melt-and-pour soap from your local craft store or make it yourself from scratch, all soap begins with this process which is known as saponification.

In the simplest of terms, soap is a type of salt. An acidic compound mixes together with a base compound and the end result is what we call soap. For making bars of soap, the base used is sodium hydroxide, commonly known as lye. If you are making liquid soap, the base compound used is called potassium hydroxide. A careful combo of the two makes a cream soap, almost like a thick pudding.

Which leads most people to the question: you mean that fats and oils are an acid? For the moment, we're talking in loose chemistry terms. I certainly don't think of olive oil as being as acid. Do you? Which is a good example of one thing you need to know - you don't have to know chemistry to make soap. I never took a chemistry class. Heck, I didn't really comprehend algebra until I reached my forties. So, don't sweat all the chemical shop talk. Here's what you need to know about how soap is made: the oils (or fats) blend together with the lye by way of a solvent (the water in the recipes) and their molecules keep smashing together until they finally bind to each other and cause a reaction called saponification - when the oils become soap.

How does soap clean? Water, by itself, isn't all that great for cleaning. Water has a tendency to bead up on surfaces instead of spreading itself out. Think of the last time you just rinsed off your dirty car without actually washing it with some sort of soap. Sure, it may have looked shiny and clean while you had it wet, but as soon as the car dried you were still able to see a dirty film on it, right? So, in other words, it didn't become clean. In super easy talk, soap molecules spread the water out and grab hold of the dirt, allowing the water to rinse the dirt away while it is still trapped inside the little bubbles of soap.

During the excavation process of ancient Babylon, clay cylinders were found with a soap - like substance inside. This shows evidence that the process of soap making was around as early as 2800 B.C. The cylinders had inscriptions describing the process of boiling fats with ashes (a primitive form of soap making).

Records reveal that the ancient Egyptians bathed on a regular basis. The Ebers papyrus, a medical document dated around 1500 B.C., describes combining alkaline salts with animal and vegetable oils to form a soap-like substance to be used for washing.

The story that sticks out in my mind the most is the Roman legend of Mount Sapo (which, by the way, gave soap its name). Women noticed that washing their clothing was easier when done in the Tiber River which was directly below Mount Sapo where ritual animal sacrifices took place. After a rainfall, a mixture of animal fats and ashes made its way down the mountain, turning into a crude form of soap along the way.

Later, early soap makers used potash, which was leached from wood ashes as their alkali base for soap making. Its results were often unpredictable, sometimes unpleasant in smell, and created soap that was more utilitarian than luxurious.

In the 1700's, a French chemist named Nicholas Leblanc invented an alkali using common salt.
During the 1800's, a Belgian chemist named Ernest Solvay discovered a process in which ammonia helped to extract the soda ash from salt efficiently. It soon became more readily available and its superiority, in turn, increased the quality of soap making.

In the 1940's, chemists discovered how to change the molecular structure of some naturally occurring substances. What they discovered was called "detergent" (to differentiate it from soap). The big advantage to detergents is that they work well in hard or cold water and can be formulated to clean specific types of dirts and stains. Modern detergents (known as syn-dets, or synthetic detergents) have become quite sophisticated and are seen in many, many forms. In fact, the majority of the cleaning products on the market are actually detergents of some type or another. Even commercial bar soaps commonly contain all or part detergents. As a result, there is a new, common definition of soap. The common definition of soap now refers to any product that bubbles and cleans, particularly if it is in a bar form.

This seems to have created the confusion regarding what real soap actually is. Hardeners, whiteners, lather boosters, chemical fragrances (sometimes with as many as five hundred separate chemical components to create their unique scent) are often found in "over the counter" store-bought "soap" or detergent bars.

This is something I have to explain on a daily basis to new customers who are wondering why they should pay five dollars for a bar of soap instead of getting a 3-pack of "soap" for two bucks at the Big Box store. First, I explain about all of the chemicals added to their cheap store soap. Then, here's my usual spiel: Your skin is natural. Our real, handmade soap is natural. But, when you use a bar that is full of chemical additions every day, your body begins saying, "hey, this doesn't belong on me. Get it off me. Get it off me." When you continue to use it, the last resort your body uses to get your attention (since you can't hear its screaming little voice) is to show up as dry skin.

Good skin care relies on moisture. The soap recipes found in this book, as well as most handmade soaps, retain all the naturally occurring glycerin - a byproduct of the soap making process. Glycerin is a humectant, meaning, it pulls moisture from the air towards your skin. Commercial soaps have had the glycerin removed so that the company can increase their profits by selling it off as a separate ingredient. It ups their profits and increases your chance of dry skin. No wonder you want to learn to make your own soap!

I can't tell you how many times I've heard the phrase, "Oh, but I can't use lye soap on my sensitive skin." Let me repeat this one more time. ALL soap begins with lye (or something just like it) and don't let anyone try to tell you differently. The chemical name for lye is sodium hydroxide. When you read the label on a bar of commercial soap, they have disguised this crucial ingredient by mashing the word with another ingredient and rebranding it. Let me explain: Sodium Tallowate is the main ingredient found in most commercial soaps. What they are actually saying is that sodium hydroxide (lye) has been mixed with tallow (rendered beef fat). In mixing these ingredients together, they have created a new word for the consumer - sodium tallowate. How clever. If you ask me, sounds pretty deceptive.

To make matters worse, Vegans all over the world have no idea they are spreading beef fat soap on their bodies every morning. Ah, the joys of American marketing!

So, what is the difference between making your own soap at home and the lye soap that our great-grandmothers made? There is a huge difference. Many people have mentioned this in conversations over the years, "My grandmother use to make soap and it would rip your hide off!" That may be true. But dear ole granny didn't have a digital scale to weigh her lye with back then, now did she? Today's modern soap maker has greater access to a wide variety of quality ingredients. Granny did not have help from modern technology to let her know exactly, down to the gram, how much lye she should use in her combination of oils. Furthermore, Granny's oils may have consisted of anything from beef fat to a whole season's worth of saved-up bacon grease drippings.

So, that is what we are going to learn to do - how to make soaps that are gentle to the skin without the addition of unnecessary chemical fillers. Wondering if you will be able to make good soap? If you can cook, you can make soap. But first, let's talk about the different types of handmade soap.

TYPES OF SOAP

Ingredients used, as well as the soap making method can result in different types of soap. This book is entirely about cold processed soaps.

Cold Process soap

In the cold process soap making method, the combination of the heat from the melted oils and the heat from the lye water provides all that is needed to "cook" the soap. In my experience, cold process creates a smoother, more attractive soap than hot process. After mixing all ingredients, the soap is poured into a mold, covered with blankets or towels, and allowed to sit undisturbed for twenty-four hours or more. Once unmolded and cut into bars, the soap must cure for the next 3 to 4 weeks. This cure time allows the bar to harden and for all lye to neutralize. In cold process soap making, sometimes you can use less water (called a discount) to speed up the drying time.

Hot Process soap

In the hot process method, once the soap has reached trace the soap maker continues to cook the soap over a source of heat. Usually a double boiler works well. The hot process method is usually used when the soap maker does not have the time to wait several weeks for their batch of soap to cure. This heating process makes it possible to use the soap right away, although waiting at least a few days is best as the soap may still be somewhat soft. When using the hot process method, usually a water discount is not used because the full amount of water in the recipe is needed during the extra cook time. Hot process soaps do not have the same smooth consistency of cold process bars and tend to have a lumpy texture at times.

Liquid Soap

Making liquid soap from scratch is very similar to making hot process soap. The soap maker uses potassium hydroxide instead of sodium hydroxide to make the batch of soap. The time to reach trace is a little longer of a wait when using potassium hydroxide and it can often mislead you into thinking trace has occurred, only to separate again. The trick is to continue the stirring process until it reaches a taffy-like state. From there, the mixture is cooked more until it reaches a somewhat clear and gel-like consistency. I always use a large Crockpot (set to low) to cook the liquid soap batch, stirring every thirty minutes. This method usually takes anywhere between three and five hours. Afterwards, the mixture is diluted with more water as well as neutralizing ingredients, allowed to cool, and eventually becomes liquid soap.

Milled Soap

Tripled Milled soap is an industry method requiring equipment. Soap is made, shredded into tiny pieces, allowed to dry, and then it is mashed and rolled under the pressure of metal rollers until it forms a paste. The paste is then put into soap molds to achieve the desire shape. Triple milled soap makes for a very hard and long-lasting bar. Hand Milled soap is the homemade version of the above method, minus all the fancy equipment. Soap is made, then grated, wetted and scented then smashed back to together. Sometimes extra water is added and the grated soap is cooked. Making soap balls is a type of hand milling.

Glycerin Soap

Here, I am going to get some complaints. I don't really care much for glycerin soap, mainly because most of the brands out there aren't much different from commercial soap and because the name is misleading. Many customers think they are buying a soap that has nothing but glycerin in it and that the soap never saw a spot of lye. Not true. Made from scratch handmade soap contains all the skin-loving glycerin you could ever want. While you can make translucent soaps at home, it is a juggling act that requires alcohol and sugar. My main point is that melt-and-pour soap that you find in the craft stores might be pretty to look at and quick to melt in the microwave but, in my experience, it just doesn't compare to real handmade soap. If you attempt to make real glycerin soap from scratch using the alcohol and sugar method, that is an entirely different story.

Animal or Vegetable?

Whether or not to use lard (from pigs) or beef tallow in your soap in completely up to you. I must admit that I don't have much experience in using animal products because I have always wanted our soaps to appeal to Vegetarians and Vegans. However, many soap makers brag about what a hard and high quality bar that lard makes. Lard is affordable and easy to obtain from any grocery store. While you will only find a few recipes in this book that contain animal products, a simple internet search should yield plenty more results. Or, use one of the many online soap lye calculators available to tweak some of the vegetable oil recipes found here by replacing ingredients such as shortening with lard.

SOAP MAKING TERMS & EQUIPMENT

Sap Value

Saponification value. The amount of sodium hydroxide (or potassium hydroxide) in milligrams required to saponify 1 gram of oil. It is the measurement of the average molecular weight of all the fatty acids present.

Saponification

The process or reaction of combining a carrier oil (fat) with an alkali (such as sodium hydroxide) to produce a salt (soap) and a free alcohol (glycerin).

Seize

The unexpected thickening and hardening of the soap mixture during the soap making process. Most often caused when adding synthetic fragrance oils to the mixture. However, certain essential oils can also speed up the process and cause seizure such as clove oil or cinnamon oil.

Sodium Hydroxide

A strong alkaline compound, NaOH, used to produce hard bars of soap.

Superfatted

The addition of extra oils or butters in an attempt to have these oils completely blended into, but not saponified within the finished soap. These excess oils contribute to the moisturizing properties of the soap.

Synthetic

Not of natural origin, artificially produced or manufactured.

Trace

A point in soap making where the mixture reaches a certain consistency or thickness, similar to pudding; most noticeable when the soap is drizzled upon itself and leaves a mark before disappearing back into the mixture.

TOOLS & ESSENTIAL SUPPLIES

Let's go over the simple and inexpensive equipment you will need to begin the art of soap making.

SCALE:

This is perhaps the most important piece of equipment you will need to begin making soap. If you have a digital scale, that's great. If not, try to borrow one until you can fit it into your budget. Precise measurement of ingredients is what creates a superior bar of soap. Measuring by weight, instead of volume, gives you complete control over what your finished product becomes. You can find quality digital scales at your local office supply store for as little as $20 to as much as $300 or more. More expensive does not always mean better, though, as long as the scale does what it was meant to do. Melted carrier oils and some essential oils can take their toll on a scale over time. I've learned a trick over the years on how to keep a scale like new for a long time. When you purchase your scale, slide it into a gallon size (larger if you need it) plastic, ziplock bag and seal the end with packing tape. If you spill oils on the scale it won't matter – it's protected. If you obtain a scale that won't fit in a bag, try wrapping it in a clear wrap such as saran wrap. The key to using clear wrap is to get it tight enough where a wrinkle doesn't prevent you from seeing the digital numbers but loose enough so that the pressure doesn't register as any weight on the scale. I currently use two scales: an eleven pound scale in a plastic bag and a larger thirty pound scale wrapped in clear wrap.

LYE RESISTANT POT:

An 8-quart pot is a good size to begin with. Be sure to use either stainless steel or an enamel-covered pot. Aluminum pots are NOT meant for soap making, as it reacts with the lye. This will be the main pot you will use for mixing all the ingredients together when you reach the point of beginning your soap batch. It can also be used to melt your base carrier oils.

RUBBER GLOVES:

Wear these to protect yourself during the soap making process, as lye will irritate and burn the skin if you allow it to come in direct contact. Surgical gloves are pretty useless when it comes to soap making. Instead, buy the yellow gloves, the dishwashing kind. These also wear out over time. The hardware store usually carries a heavy-duty version of rubber gloves. My heavy green pair lasts around six months, and this is with making soap five days a week. The yellow, everyday variety usually last me about a month or so.

GOGGLES:

An ounce of prevention is worth a pound of cure and there is nothing more precious than your eyesight. Wear goggles while dealing with your lye and mixing your soap. Don't question it, just do it.

PLASTIC PITCHER:

Thick plastic is preferable for mixing the lye/water solution. One with a pouring spout is ideal. You can usually find these for as little as $1 or $2 at discount stores. If the $2 one is sturdier, then by all means, splurge. You don't want the kind where the handle bends with the pressure of heavy water. To protect your family, take a large, black marker and write "LYE PITCHER – DO NOT USE" on the outside of the container. Never reuse a pitcher for anything else once you have used it as a lye pitcher. I don't care how clean you think it looks. Better safe than sorry.

LARGE SPOONS:

Long, heavy plastic ones are a good choice for mixing the lye/water solution and for mixing ingredients into your main pot. Some people will use wooden spoons for the actual soap making, but they can become a little splintery over time.

2 CANDY THERMOMETERS:

One is for the lye/water solution; the other for your melted oils. One method in making soap is getting these two mixtures the same, or very close to the same, temperature before pouring the lye/water solution into your melted oils. (We will cover this in more detail later).

SOAP MOLDS:

You can use something as simple as a shoebox lined with a thick garbage bag or even a hard plastic storage box that you have greased and lined with wax paper or freezer paper. This master mold will create your soap "loaf" or "log" from which you will later cut out your bars of soap.

A new kitty litter pan works well. Wooden boxes make great soap molds. Wooden molds are all I use now and I don't think I'd ever go back to using something else. Whenever I purchase a brand new wooden soap mold, I rub the entire surface down with Vaseline. I know it's not that natural but it really does help to protect the wood. After the Vaseline has sunk in, I rub down the wooden mold with something like canola a couple of times, letting it sink in between coats. This lengthens the life of the mold and makes it much easier to get the soap out. For wood molds, I always line with heavy garbage bags. If you have made several batches and your wood mold is getting a little dry, don't be afraid to grease it down from time to time.

WAX PAPER or FREEZER PAPER:

As mentioned above, it is used in lining hard plastic molds, making un-molding your soap a much easier task. While I am still a fan of hefty lawn bags, I understand that many people like to use wax paper or freezer paper to line their molds because they can fold clean lines into the corners. Trash bags do have a tendency to leave a wrinkle here and there, usually at the ends of the soap.

STICK BLENDER:

Oh, what an invention! The first time I made soap I stirred it with a spoon. The second time I used a stick blender. I never looked back! These handy little gadgets can make the difference in your soap coming to trace and being ready to pour into molds in as little as 10 minutes versus an hour or more of hand stirring. Additionally, a stick blender ensures better blending of all the ingredients. They can range anywhere between $9 and $35 and up. I found that my "cheap" stick blender outlasted the more expensive model by more than two years. But the cheap ones seem to be getting harder and harder to find. The last two blenders I purchased were at Kmart and cost about $29 each. Yes, I paid the $2 extra for the two-year replacement insurance policy on them. The previous month I had a stick blender go out just weeks after the one-year warranty expired!

OLD TOWELS OR BLANKETS:

These are used as insulation for covering your molds during the "cooking" process. Cover molds with several layers of towels or a folded blanket. Allowing the heat to stay trapped in the mold overnight lets the soap go thoroughly through the gel-phase.

COFFEE GRINDER:

You can also opt for the old-fashioned mortar and pestle. These are for finely grinding any herbs and botanicals you would like to add to your soaps, as well as for powdering oatmeal.

LYE:

In the first edition of this book, I directed soap makers to go to the local grocery store and buy 100% Red Devil lye. But, it just cannot be found anymore. It seems that the makers of illegal drugs use it in their labs, which is why it was pulled from supermarket shelves. If you live in an area where it is still available, that's great. Just be sure it is 100% sodium hydroxide. Regular drain cleaners contain small elements of metal and other substances and cannot be used in soap making. One option is to look for other soap makers in your area to find out where they obtain their lye. Chemical companies sell it in fifty pound bags (this is how I purchase it) but that may be more than you are willing to store. Other soapers in your community might co-op with you and split the lye (and the cost). Whether you decide on the full bag or to split it among friends, the lye cannot be stored in the bag in came in after you open it. It will need to be transferred to something like a clean, plastic bucket with a well fitted lid. Sodium hydroxide can also be purchased online from some soap making suppliers. It is almost always sold in two pound quantities. Anything over that weight and an expensive hazmat fee is required. See the resources at the back of the book for suppliers.

Lye safety is important. Accidentally ingesting it can cause severe internal damage or even death. If this happens, contact emergency services immediately. Lye is corrosive. If you splash a few drops on your arm, wash immediately and apply apple cider vinegar. The vinegar is said to neutralize it when it comes in contact with the skin. If a spill gets on your clothing, remove them right away and wash the area that came in contact. Large amounts of water is the key to removing all of the lye from the skin. When your skin no longer has a slick feel to it, you can then treat the area as you would any other injury or burn. If in doubt, consult your physician.

If you are mindful that you are using a powerful substance, and use your goggles and gloves, then you should be fine with handling the lye for your soap making. If you have small children or pets that can run under your feet, it is best to shut the kitchen door or put up a baby gate before beginning your project. I've heard many soap makers say that they make soap after the children have gone to bed.

WATER:

Distilled or spring water is usually preferred, but many soap makers use water directly from the tap. Only you will be able to determine if this is best for your use, depending on the quality of your local water supply. Soap makers that are more "rustic" like to collect rainwater for the process. I have even heard of Northern soap makers bringing in snow from outside and letting it melt. Water works as your solvent – the thing you will dissolve the lye in and what allows the lye to reach all the molecules of the soap making oils.

CARRIER-BASE OILS:

Some of the oils used in soap making are: olive oil, vegetable shortening, coconut oil, palm oil, cocoa butter, sunflower oil, safflower oil, canola oil, jojoba, and castor oil. Lard and beef tallow are used by many soap makers. Coconut is almost always used for creating fluffy lather. Olive oil is popular because it has a moisturizing, slippery lather. A well balanced soap recipe takes the best of different oils for their unique properties and combines them.

ADDITIVES:

Soap isn't just for getting clean. Some love it for the fragrance it imparts; others make soaps that include herbs that are known for their healing powers or by using ingredients that are known for promoting healthy skin. Some additives are used for their exfoliating properties to aid in removing dead skin cells. There are several other ingredients you can add to soap to make a gentler, more emollient bar. Honey is quite popular in many soaps as well as several types of clays, extra added glycerin, goat or cow's milk, powdered milk, and even such luxuries as pureed cucumbers, mashed bananas, and egg yolks. I have become rather fond of powdered honey because it is less messy and takes very little to use.

ESSENTIAL OILS:

Essential oils come from plants and are used to fragrance soaps and other toiletries, especially if you want natural ingredients. Essential oils are also what is used in aromatherapy and have different healing values. For example: lavender is for relaxation; peppermint or spearmint energizes; sweet orange lifts the spirits; tea tree is cleansing and antifungal, etc. (See back of book for a short guide to using essential oils).

FRAGRANCE OILS:

They may not have aromatherapeutic value like essential oils do (at least on a medicinal level), but fragrance oils come in a wider variety of scents. These are man-made fragrances of a chemical compound and are often the main ingredient for creating perfumes. Some examples of fragrance oils that have gone beyond natural scents are: cucumber melon, mango, strawberry, sweet pea....well, you get the picture. Be sure to purchase fragrance oils from a reputable supplier who can let you know whether or not their oils are skin safe. Many fragrance oils are made specifically for candles and incense and should not be used on the skin. Furthermore, not all artificial fragrances work well in the soap making process. Some have a tendency to "seize" your batch of soap, meaning, the soap becomes hard in the pot before you have time to pour it into the mold. Unfortunately, the only way to tell if fragrance oil is going to work well is trial-and-error.

HERBS & BOTANICALS:

Many times, if you add the same botanical to a soap as the essential oil you used, it helps to "anchor" the scent and make it last longer. Oatmeal is known to be soothing. Oil of cinnamon, used to stimulate the beard in shaving soaps, can be an irritant for those with sensitive skin. Adding poppy seeds or almond meal can act as an exfoliant. Only use dried herbs, never fresh. Fresh herbs don't care much for lye and can make a messy goo in your batch of soap. Also, fresh herbs are more likely to rot and decay inside your bar of soap. There are some exceptions to the rule. Some fruit and vegetables, usually those with a high water content, can add special properties to your soap. Pureed cucumbers, strawberries, carrot, and tomato are four ingredients that are often used in soap. However, the soaps containing these fruits and vegetables don't usually last as long.

COLORING:

There are many options for adding color to your batches of soap. Powdered clove or cinnamon adds a warm, earth tone; powdered parsley brings out a pale green tone, as does powdered peppermint. Just keep in mind that using natural colorants usually imparts some of the fragrance and/or qualities of those additives. In addition, there are many powdered pigments and micas on the market made just for soap making that come in a wide variety of colors: bright blues, pink tones, violets, yellows....even black. Just remember that a little colorant usually goes a long way so experiment as needed. Food coloring rarely works and the results are unreliable, especially when dealing with reds. They are a better fit for coloring melt-and-pour soap. The lye reaction changes something when you use food coloring and yellow seems to be the only one that gives fair results. Never use candle dyes or clothing dye in your soaps. Not only do they contain other ingredients that may not be gentle to your skin, but your white washcloths won't be too happy with you, either.

CARRIER OILS – SOAP MAKING OILS

Before listing the oils, let's discuss a term known as superfatting. Superfatting means that you have used less than the amount of lye needed to turn all of the oils into soap, leaving unsaponified oils throughout your bar to aid in moisturizing the skin. Some soap makers do this while formulating their recipe; others add a luxury oil towards the end of the soap making process. Adding the oil in at the end helps to ensure that the oil you have selected is the one that is actually the "extra oil". All of the recipes found in this book are superfatted at either 4 or 5%. Some soap makers use the full amount of lye in the beginning then add the luxury oil at trace. If you would like to further superfat any of the recipes in this book, just don't go overboard. Adding an ounce extra shea butter, cocoa butter, etc., shouldn't pose any problems for you. Too much superfatting and the soap does not stick together; it separates.

Sweet Almond Oil is often used for superfatting soaps. It is a great moisturizer, makes a stable lather and helps condition the skin. Add 1 ounce per pound of fats to your soap batch at trace.

Apricot Kernel Oil is often used for superfatting. It is also a good moisturizer and helps condition the skin. Use one or two ounces in every pound of fat at trace.

Avocado Oil is a great moisturizer and is often used for superfatting soaps. Avocado oil contains vitamins A, D, and E, which makes it healing as well as moisturizing. Try it in a gentle baby soap. Use up to 30% as base oil.

Canola Oil is a good moisturizer but is less saturated than other fats, so it can be slow to saponify. Use it in place of more expensive oils like olive. Mix with other saturated fats to speed up saponification. Use as a base oil up to 50%.

Castor Oil is often used to superfat. It attracts and holds moisture to the skin. Use it in combination with other vegetable oils to produce a nice hard bar of soap. You can add a bit at trace for superfatting or add it to other oils at a rate of no more than 30% in the beginning of the soap making process.

Cocoa butter is used to make soaps harder. When used in soap as a superfatting oil it acts to lay down a protective layer that holds the moisture to the skin, so it is an excellent skin softener. It has a natural chocolate scent but it is also available in unscented versions. You can use about one ounce to a pound at trace, or as much as 15% of your total base oils, depending on your preference.

Coconut Oil makes soaps lather beautifully but can be drying when it makes up a large portion of your soaps' fats. It will make a very hard, white bar of soap with abundant lather. It easily lathers in very hard water, even seawater. Coconut oil is a saturated fat. Use it at a percentage of no more than 20-30% in your base oils.

Grapeseed Oil is a lightweight oil that absorbs into the skin quickly without leaving a heavy greasy feeling. Used in soaps as a superfatting oil. Use one ounce per pound at trace.

Hazelnut Oil is an excellent moisturizer for soaps. It is low in saturated fatty acids, so use other more saturated fats to lessen your trace time and yield a harder bar. Recommended maximum usage - 20% of total oils.

Jojoba helps to promote a stable lather and is good at conditioning skin. Because of its expense, it is usually used to superfat soap batches or in shampoo bars. It is an excellent emollient for skin conditions like psoriasis, because it has a chemical composition very close to the skin's own sebum. It is suitable for all skin types, beneficial for spotty and acne conditions, and good for sensitive and oily skin. When using jojoba in soap, limit its usage to one or two ounces per pound at trace. Jojoba naturally accelerates tracing in soap recipes. Used as a Superfatting oil.

Kukui Nut Oil is native to Hawaii and is high in linoleic acid. It is quickly absorbed into the skin. Excellent for skin conditioning after sun exposure, as well as for acne, eczema, and psoriasis. It offers just the right amount of lubrication without leaving a greasy feeling. For soap making, use 2 tablespoons added to 5 lbs of soap at trace just before incorporating the essential oils to add richness to the soap.

Lard is made from pig fat much like bacon fat. Its advantages are that it is cheap, easily obtainable, and makes a nice lathery, white bar of soap. This fat should be combined with vegetable oils such as coconut or palm to compensate for the lard's shortcomings. Without other oils, it can tend to be soft and not work very well in cold water. Use it as a base oil. Recommended at 70% maximum of total oils.

Macadamia is a luxurious and slightly expensive oil, best used for superfatting. It has a long shelf life so it can be purchased in quantity for a good price. Use 1 ounce per pound at trace.

Mango butter is extracted from the mango fruit. It is a yellowish oil and has almost no scent. It is a great moisturizer and should be used to superfat batches. Can be used at up to 15% of base or as a superfatting agent at 5% at trace.

Olive Oil is excellent as a base oil in soaps, either in whole (Castile soap) or in part. Avoid extra virgin olive oil. It is great for cooking but not for soap making. The lower the grades are best. If you are making an especially mild soap or baby soap, use Olive oil. Use as a base oil up to 100% .

Palm Oil makes a hard bar that cleans well and is also mild. It is a good substitute for tallow in all-vegetable soaps. The quality of Palm oil is far superior to other vegetable oils that are filler oils. Palm oil is universal and used in many expensive luxury soaps. Use it as a Base oil at 20 - 30%.

Palm Kernel Oil makes a soap that is very hard and lathers well. It has most of the same qualities as palm oil. Use it as a base oil at 20-30%

Safflower Oil is an unsaturated oil and should be used in combination with palm, coconut, or a similar oil. It is valuable for its moisturizing properties. Use it as Base oil up to 60%. 20% of total is more highly recommended.

Shea butter is a wonderful superfatting agent and contains a large percentage of ingredients that do not react with the lye, thus remaining in the soap to nourish your skin. Use it with your base at up to 20% of your total oils or as a superfatting agent at 1 2/3 tablespoons per 5 pounds of oils added at trace. Shea Butter comes two different ways – in its natural state and refined. Natural shea butter is yellow in color and has a nutty scent to it. Refined shea butter has undergone a cleaning process and is white and odorless. Which one you decide to use depends totally on preference and whether or not you think the natural shea will interfere with the final scent of your soap.

Sunflower Oil is a less expensive alternative to olive oil. It contains Vitamin E, so it naturally resists going rancid (Vitamin E is a preservative). Try to avoid using more than about 15-20% sunflower oil. It can make your soaps take longer to trace and to harden. Use as a Base oil up to 20%.

Vegetable shortening is normally made out of soybean oil. It is cheap, readily available, and produces a mild but stable lather. Use it in combination with other exotic or moisturizing oils. Use this as half of your fats to keep costs down. It is a good filler. It makes a very hard white bar when used alone or when mixed with other oils. Use vegetable shortening as a base oil or combine it with other, harder oils for better results. Recommend use as base up to 50% of total oils. If you are a purist, look for organic or non-GMO (genetically modified) soybean shortening. Many suppliers carry both types.

The following chart is known as a saponification chart. Basically, this means that it takes a certain amount of lye to turn a specific oil into soap. Each oil has its own characteristics and a special saponification value. The sap value of each oil measures the needed amount of sodium hydroxide (lye) required to turn that particular oil into soap. Confused? Let's make it easier. Multiply the amount of oil you are using (in ounces) by the value for that oil found on the chart. That total is the amount of lye (sodium hydroxide) needed. If using a combination of oils, multiply for each and add all the sums for the total of all the oils used in your recipe.

Example: 32 ozs. of vegetable shortening x 0.136 = 4.35 ounces of lye needed.
To calculate water/liquid: Use 6 ozs of liquid per pound (16 ozs) of oil/fat.
Example: 32 ozs of total oils/fats ÷ 16 = 2 x 6 = 12 oz of liquid.

Later in this book you will find a number of recipes where everything is already calculated for you. While you are still in the beginning phases of learning to make soap, don't let the saponification chart confuse you, as you will be provided with plenty of recipes to keep you busy.

SAPONIFICATION CHART

Oil	Sap Value
Almond Oil, Sweet	.137
Apricot Kernel Oil	.134
Avocado Oil	.132
Canola Oil	.123
Castor Oil	.127
Cocoa Butter	.136
Coconut Oil	.178
Grapeseed Oil	.134
Hazelnut Oil	.135
Jojoba Oil	.065
Kukui Nut Oil	.135
Lard	.138
Macadamia Nut Oil	.137
Mango Butter	.134
Olive Oil	.133
Palm Kernel Oil	.155
Palm Oil	.139
Safflower Oil	.135
Shea Butter	.126
Shortening (veg)	.136
Sunflower Oil	.134

MAKING SOAP – THE STANDARD INSTRUCTIONS

So far we have covered what soap is, the oils used in soap making, lye safety, additional ingredients, the types of soap, supplies you will need, and ways to color and scent your soap. Now, let's move on to the nitty gritty – the basic instructions on how to make a batch of soap.

To begin, I am going to take you through the standard process of soap making; the same instructions everyone follows when they learn the process. The entire first section of this book deals with the standard soap making directions and recipes. Later in the book we will discuss a faster way to make a lot of soap in a short amount of time. But, first things first – let's just focus on how to make soap. You must learn to cook before thinking about catering a banquet!

We talked a little about lye safety. Never put your hands or fingers in the lye water to check the temperature. You are dealing with a chemical mixture that will cause a chemical burn and can be fatal if swallowed. Keep lye and your lye mixture away from children and pets. NEVER add water to lye. The proper procedure is to add the lye to the water.

The best way I've found to remember which one is the right order is something I read several years ago: "the snow falls on the lake". Adding water to lye can cause an eruption. Years ago, there was a popular soap making book that gave the instructions in reverse and caused quite a bit of conflict and talk among soap makers. Turns out it was the fault of the book editor who changed the order of the words. Still, the author of the book was never regarded as a serious soap maker again. So, once again, always add the lye to the water, exactly in this order!

Put on your latex gloves and safety goggles when you are ready to make your lye/water mixture. When you mix lye into water, it will heat up right away, jumping to over 200 degrees. Many people choose to mix their lye solution outside or perhaps in the garage. I've always kept my plastic lye pitcher in the sink while mixing, making sure to hold my head back away from the pitcher the whole time - away from the mixing process and away from the fumes. Wearing a surgical mask while mixing lye water is a good and safe practice to protect your lungs.

STEP ONE:

Set out all utensils you will be using. Measure any essential oils/fragrance oils you will be adding to your soap as well as any herbs, botanicals, colorants, etc.

STEP TWO:

Line your soap mold(s) and have it ready. Once your mixture becomes soap, you will have to move quickly and this needs to be ready.

STEP THREE:

Time to put on your gloves, mask, and goggles. Using your scale, measure into a Pyrex cup or disposable plastic cup the amount of lye you will need for the recipe you will be using. Set the lye aside. Now, with your lye pitcher on it set your scale back to zero and measure in the amount of water you will need into your lye pitcher. Set the pitcher in the sink (or outside) and slowly pour the lye into the water and gently stir with your hard plastic spoon until the lye dissolves. The water will be cloudy at first then turn clear. Set your lye mixture aside in a safe location where it cannot be spilled by children, pets or you.

STEP FOUR:

Measure out the oils you plan to use in your recipe directly into your soap pot. Melt them on medium to medium-low heat. Do not overheat. You want the oils to simply be melted – you are not making French fries! When melted, set your pot aside. Both the melted oils and your lye/water solution need to go through a cooling down period. Get out your candy thermometers and place one in each of your mixtures. You are waiting for both the melted oils and your lye/water mixture to reach the neighborhood of 100 – 120 degrees. Many books will tell you they have to be the EXACT same temperature or the process will not work. Nonsense! As long as you stay within the temperatures we talked about above and they are close to the same, everything will be fine.

In fact, this is something that stumped me the first time I made soap. I was wondering how I would be able to get both at the exact same temperature since they were two completely different compounds. A cool or warm water bath, depending on what you are trying to achieve, is often helpful. If my lye water is cooling down much faster than my oils, I will put the pot of hot oils into a sink filled with cold water until the temperatures reach the acceptable range.

STEP FIVE:

Plug in your stick blender. Now that both your melted oils and your lye water have reached the right temperatures, slowly pour your lye water into your oils. Immerse your stick blender and begin blending. If you have a small batch of soap, you may need to tilt your pot just a bit in order to make the mixture deep enough to avoid splattering. Keep your stick blender deep and do not try pulling it up to the surface while on, as this could cause the mixture to splash. If any soap mixture does happen to get on your skin, wash immediately with cold water and vinegar. The way I use my stick blender is by blending a few moments, then turning it off and simply stirring with it, then blending with it again. This helps prolong the life of your stick blender's motor, reducing overheating and overwork.

Many soap makers wait until trace (when the soap mixture reaches a thin pudding-like stage) before adding colorant. I add my color shortly after adding the lye mixture to the oils. Often, I will add them to the melted base oils even before I pour in the lye water. I feel this saves you some much needed time just in case your soap traces too quickly and you run out of time.

STEP SIX:

When you first mixed your lye water and oils, you noticed that the mixture still looked like an oily soup. As trace begins to occur, the mixture turns opaque and begins to thicken. As you see this slight thickening start, you will be able to take your stick blender (turned off) and drag it across the top of your mixture. If it leaves a line or "blob" for a few seconds before falling back into the mixture, you have reached trace. The consistency is something like thin pudding. But keep in mind that you will want to follow step seven below before a thick trace prevents you from adding in the "good stuff".

STEP SEVEN:

Add your essential oils/fragrance oils and botanicals and stir well. Work quickly. If your soap becomes too thick, you will not be able to pour it into the molds. Sometimes fragrance oils, being man-made chemicals of various compounds, can cause what is known as "seizure". This is when the soap suddenly hardens in the pot within just a few seconds and pouring into the molds is no longer a possibility. Try to choose fragrance oils that have been tested for use in cold process soap making. Most essential oils do not cause such sudden seizure unless using too much. For your first batch try using real essential oils (such as lavender) or a simple, unscented batch.

STEP EIGHT:

Pour your traced soap mixture into the mold. You can use the oven (turned off) to place your molds in if you don't plan to use it until the next day. You can also take a large cardboard box, larger and taller than your soap mold and turn it upside down over your mold. Now is the time you wrap the box in your old towels or blankets to retain the heat. Here is the hard part - leave the box alone until the next day. What is going on in your mold, under the box is called "gel phase". This is when the lye is continuing to work on your soap mixture, heating it up until it takes on a gelled look, similar to Vaseline. Slowly, it cools back down and the process completes itself.

STEP NINE:

24 hours later, remove the box and put your latex gloves back on. At this point, the soap may still have a bit of a "sting" to it. Turn your mold upside down on your countertop and press the back a bit to try to get the soap to release from the mold. It can be similar to removing ice from ice trays. If you have a stubborn batch that does not seem to want to come out of the mold, place the mold in the freezer for about an hour then try again. If you are using a wooden mold lined with heavy plastic (my preference), gravity will take over in a few minutes after turning the mold upside down. Once unmolded, slowly peel off your freezer/wax paper and slice your loaf of soap into the size bars that you would like to have. Remember, this step occurs on the <u>second</u> day.

STEP TEN:

This is the aging process. Place your soap in a well-ventilated area away from air conditioners or heaters. A shelf lined with wax paper works quite well. Leave the soap alone for at least 4 to 6 weeks. During this curing time, the soap's PH lowers, giving you a milder bar. Also, during this time, the water is naturally dehydrating from your soap and creating a harder, longer lasting bar of soap.

The Curing Process

Cold processed soaps need time to cure and age before they can be labeled and sold. The Hot Process method of making soap does make for a bar that can be sold right away. However, their look and feel is not the same as cold process. Cold process soaps are usually smooth and hard bars of soap but require more patience because of cure.

The explanation for why the bars need time to cure is easy to understand. We mentioned hot process above. This is when the soap maker continues to cook each batch of soap over a heat source, speeding up the saponification process (the lye) and continues to evaporate the water. With cold process soaps, nature takes care of the curing process by allowing the soaps sit out in the open.

When the soap is made, the fatty ingredients (coconut, olive, shea, soybean) are blended with sodium hydroxide (lye) along with essential oils and color and spices or herbs. When the lye (diluted in water) mixes with the molecules of the fatty oils – what you end up with is soap. However, the soaping process, known as saponification, continues over the next couple of weeks. As the bars of soap are allowed to sit out in the air, the lye works its way out of the batch and the water continues to evaporate a little more each day.

A bar of soap CAN be used after only two weeks of curing. It won't harm you. But, softer soaps melt away faster in the shower or tub. When your bars of soap are allowed to cure a full four to six weeks, the end result is a very hard bar of soap. The basic rule is – the longer it sits, the harder it gets, and the longer it lasts.

When you cut your soaps into bars, spread the bars out a bit. A slight space between each one is enough to allow air to reach all sides of the bar. But when the bars are crammed against each other it makes it harder for the water in the bars of soap to evaporate. Room temperature is best. Some customers with little space have even told me that they place the bars on trays and slide the trays under the bed with a small fan running in the room when they are at home. Shelves in the laundry room work well as a curing space for your soaps too. No other options? Clean off a shelf in your closet. True, there won't be as much air circulating in there but the soaps will still cure and your clothes will smell amazing and everyone will ask about it.

Another reason why some soaps need a longer cure time has to do with their ingredients. Soaps that contain honey usually feel more 'oily' in the beginning. If you label your honey soaps too soon it will leave an oily stain on the label.

If you follow the simple rules of how to cure your soap, it

will make all the difference in the feedback you receive from customers. Their bars will last longer and they will come back for more. After all, you wouldn't want to buy cheese that hadn't been aged properly. Curing soap is similar.

How to Cut Soap Into Bars

The number one question I receive on our bulk soap loaf site is, "How do I cut the loaf of soap into bars? What do I use?" For years, I have used a wooden miter box and a pastry scraper to cut the soap. If you choose to use a knife to cut with, make sure it is large enough to slice all the way through the loaf of soap - but, too large of a blade or too thick of a blade can cut away more soap than is needed.

If possible, invest in one of the better pastry scrapers, the kind with the firm or wooden handle attached. They also come as one piece of metal with a curve on the end for the handle - but this type tends to warp over time. They are, however, more affordable – usually only about $6.95. The better scrapers should run around $15 and up.

The reason I chose a wooden miter box as a guide for cutting a soap is simple — it can be altered. Most miter boxes do not have grooves that go all the way down to the floor of the miter box. With a wooden model, you can insert a saw into the straight cut (you do not want to cut your soap on an angle for regular bars) and finish sawing the groove down to the floor of the miter box. This insures that your bars of soap will be cut all the way through.

Now is the time to decide how wide you want your bars to be. Most people choose to cut their soaps into a one-inch thickness. I cut our soap bars 1.25 inches thick, which gives us 12 bars from a loaf of soap. When you decide your thickness, measure over from the straight cut and make a mark on top of the miter box to the right of the guide.

So, slide the soap loaf into the miter box from the left and bring the edge of the soap over to the mark you've made on the top of the miter box. Now, take your pastry scraper and start from the back side and begin sliding the blade into the soap loaf in a rocking down motion until the blade falls into the straight groove closest to you. You have now cut your first bar of soap off of your soap loaf. Repeat until finished. Save any leftover soap pieces for the kitchen or use as soap samples for friends.

Calculating Sold Mold Volume

Let's say you've made all the recipes in this book and want to move on to smaller or larger batches. You have a box in the garage that would be perfect for a soap mold but have no idea how to figure out how much soap it will hold. Here is how you do it.

There are so many things that can be used for soap molds – cat litter boxes (new, of course), shoeboxes, and cigar boxes – okay, you get the point, boxes are great for soap molds. Once you decide on the exact size of mold you prefer, a wooden box makes an excellent mold as it is sturdy and durable.

Thoroughly lining your mold of choice with a thick trash bag will prevent leaks and allows the finished soap to slip out easily. My first experience with wooden soap molds was of the hinged variety – where the sides would drop down for easy removal of the soap. However, I found that when the mold is well oiled and lined with a trash bag it is unnecessary to have hinged or removable sides. The soap slips easily out of a solid wooden box when it is lined properly.

So, how to figure out how much soap base you need for a box or mold you already have? The calculations are simple. Mold length x mold width x depth x .38 = ounces of soap making oils that will fit in your mold.

Some people fill their molds all the way to the top. I prefer to leave a little room as far as the depth goes. For example, if I want my soap bars to be 3 inches high, I would favor a soap mold that is at least 3 ½ inches deep. It is a personal preference.

Let's try an example with an imaginary box you've found in

the attic. The box is 10 inches long, 3 inches wide, and 4 inches deep. Let us presume you only want to fill the box 3 inches deep, instead of all the way full. This calculation for soap volume would be –

10 x 3 x 3 = 90

90 x .38 = 34.2

So, now we know that your soap mold will hold 34.2 ounces of soap making oils. This calculation for volume includes the amount of water and fragrance or essential oils that are normally used when making a batch of soap.

This math calculation will allow you to determine how much soap formula you will need for any square or rectangular container you are considering using as a soap mold.

Dealing With Soda Ash

Soda ash – as your soap ages, you may notice a powdery substance on the surface of the soap. This is nothing to worry about and is usually seen on the surface of the soap that was exposed to air while still in the mold. It can be scraped off of your aged soap or simply washed off. Some soap makers even find it attractive - others do their best to avoid it. One way to help prevent soda ash is to cover the surface of your mold with greased wax paper or plastic wrap before placing your box and towels over the mold.

Making Colored Swirls in Soap

Over time, I have noticed that the customers in our soap store reached for the brightly colored or the swirled (some call it "marbled") bars of soap. Once you get the hang of making soap and have a few batches under your belt, your next rite of passage is learning how to swirl two colors of soap together. Swirling is achieved by beginning the soap making process, removing some of the batch and coloring it, then adding it back to the rest of the batch. Sounds scary, huh?

The first thing you need to know about creating swirls is that you do NOT want to discount the water in your soap recipes. Using the full amount of water a batch will withstand gives you a little extra time to work with two bowls of soap. All of the recipes in this book have a slight water discount. When you decide to attempt swirling, increase the water amount in your recipe to a full 15 ounces when you mix your lye solution. Most recipes found here are in the 13.5 ounce water range. The second thing that is important is temperature. The 100° Fahrenheit point is pretty good for mixing colors. Moving quickly and having no distractions around you is important for swirling. If the phone rings in the middle of the process, let it ring.

For your first attempt, don't try to create two colors. Leave one natural and color the other. First, you are going to have a second bowl ready with a little color already in the bottom of the bowl. If using a powdered color, I always put in a small splash of water – just enough to get the powder wet. This makes it easier to blend with the soap you are going to pour into the bowl. Then, you are going to begin making the soap batch as you normally would, according to the standard soap making directions. What you are looking for is called light trace, that very moment when you know the oils have fully incorporated but you are not at that full pudding-like stage yet. Immediately pour part of the lightly traced batch into the bowl with the color, usually about one-third or one-fourth of the batch and begin stirring with your stick blender or with a whisk. When colored, quickly go back to your larger batch of uncolored soap to see if it needs a few more whirls with the blender.

From here, I usually take a small portion of the colored batch and drizzle it in the bottom of the mold. Then, when fully traced, I pour in the larger, uncolored batch. Immediately, take the rest of the colored soap and pour it in a wavy, zigzag pattern into the uncolored soap that is in the mold. Some will sink down; some of the color will remain on the surface. But, to further the effect, take a stick (wooden kabob skewers work well) and, starting at one end of the loaf of soap, insert the stick straight into the batch. From there you drag it through to the other end of the loaf, going back and forth a few times. Start on one side of the mold, go to the end of the mold, drag it through the middle of the batch, to the other end again, and then repeat on the other side of the mold. From there, you can go the opposite direction a few times. This will make little peaks of swirled color throughout the loaf of soap. That's all there is to it.

Okay. You may be confused right now. So, let me tell you an easier way to begin swirling two colors together - a second method. After you have thoroughly mixed the colored batch in the bowl, go back to your bigger portion and make sure it has come to trace. Then, dump the colored portion into the pan in one single motion. Don't try to get fancy, just one big "plop" into the center. Now, carry the whole batch over to your mold and pour it in. The colored portion will spread out as you pour. This method is a little more subtle than the first method and creates more of a marbled look than a starkly colored swirl.

But, if you think it will be easier to learn how to swirl by beginning with this example, start there. Attempt the harder one on your next batch. Trust me; it's easier if you read these instructions a couple of times. Run your finger along a table in a wavy, zigzag pattern and the directions should magically click in your head in an, "oh, I get it," moment.

THE SOAP RECIPES

There are as many different ways to make soap as there are to bake a cake; maybe more. The recipes in this section use a variety of soaping oils. Keep this in mind and read the recipes carefully - the lye quantities are different for every recipe. Each recipe instructs you to refer back to the standard soap making instructions, rather than repeating them over and over here.

When you find a recipe that you really like, start experimenting with different ways to fragrance it. Get creative with your colors, your herbs, your scents, your additives. Take a deep breath; find your courage and experiment.

All of the recipes in this book are based on using two pounds, twelve ounces of base carrier oils. I have found this to be a good sized recipe to handle in an 8-quart pot. If the recipe were smaller, there could possibly be a lot of splashing while you use your stick blender. This amount is just deep enough for safety's sake for the beginning soap maker. You may find that you still want to tilt your pot a bit, just to give the liquids more depth. When completely finished, each batch should yield a good dozen bars of thick soap.

Now, some may find my recipes to be heavy on the essential oils while others think they are just right. Essential oils do not impart as much scent as fragrance oils when used in small quantities in soap. If you feel the essential oils are too heavy or too heavy for your budget, feel free to cut them back. Just make sure to add in a little extra water to compensate for what you removed.

If you find the recipes in this section to be a little on the expensive side, don't worry. In the next section of the book where I explain the "Master Batch" method, the recipes use more economical oils. You can always use those recipes when you are first starting out and venture into the luxury oils when you get the hang of making soap. More information on how to use those recipes for the standard soap making instructions is found in the Master Batch chapter.

I have tried to make the recipes one to a page so that you have space for taking notes.

CHAMOMILE FACE SOAP

The high olive oil content creates a wonderful face bar. Palmarosa is a grass from Central America with a scent that reminds you of a lemony version of rose geranium. It is reported to help with wrinkles as well as being a cellular stimulant. The chamomile tea is a less expensive way of imparting its skin healing properties. If your budget allows for some chamomile essential oil (it's rather expensive), feel free to add 15 or 20 drops to this batch of soap.

28 oz. olive oil
10 oz. vegetable shortening
6 oz. coconut oil
13.2 oz. water
5.9 oz. lye
3 oz. palmarosa essential oil
1/2 oz. patchouli essential oil
Contents of one chamomile tea bag

Follow standard soap making instructions....

BABY SOAP

This version of "baby soap" is not tear-free like many of the commercial baby soaps and baby shampoos. It is simply for parents that have a need for bathing their children in more earth-friendly products. Also works great as sensitive skin soap for adults.

28 oz. olive oil
10 oz. vegetable shortening
6 oz. coconut oil
13.2 oz. water
5.8 oz. lye
1 oz. lavender essential oil

Follow standard soap making instructions....

SOLID SHAMPOO

Every soap maker must, at least once, try to make solid shampoo. Most people are amazed they have options other than the bottles of commercial hair products that line the shelves of salons and pharmacies. True, it is really more of a favorite among people with short hair. The secret is to allow your hair to air-dry. Then, you really feel how soft and silky your hair can be from a simple bar of soap.

13 oz. coconut oil
12 oz. castor oil
2 oz. cocoa butter
1 oz. jojoba oil
16 oz. olive oil
13.2 oz. water
6.1 oz. lye
1 oz. lavender essential oil
2 oz. rosemary essential oil
15 drops chamomile essential oil (optional)
1 egg yolk (no whites)

Follow standard soap making instructions....

ROSE CLAY SPA BAR

This soap is a rather indulgent bar. The beauty of the rose clay and the blend of essential oils remind you of a day at the spa. This bar has a stable lather, but not a fluffy one. However, the moisturizing properties are high and it leaves your skin feeling silky smooth. After all, look at those luxury oils in the recipe – you may want to keep this one all to yourself.

17 oz. olive oil
9 oz. palm oil
7 oz. coconut oil
8 oz. shea butter
2 oz. avocado oil
1 oz. evening primrose oil
13.2 oz. water
5.9 oz. lye
2 oz. lavender essential oil
1/2 oz. carrotseed essential oil
1/2 oz. geranium essential oil
4 teaspoons rose clay

Follow standard soap making instructions....

SANDALWOOD PATCHOULI

Sandalwood is my absolute favorite oil. But it is super, super pricey! A one ounce bottle may cost you as much as $85 plus shipping, sometimes more. But, you can always substitute fragrance oil for the real thing --- or, use part sandalwood fragrance oil and part sandalwood essential oil. Another replacement is an essential oil called Amyris, also known as "poor man's sandalwood". Whatever your wallet decides, the recipe below is based on the assumption that you're ready to make the real thing! By the way, the patchouli seems to make the sandalwood scent a bit stronger.

13 oz. coconut oil
20 oz. olive oil
2 oz. castor oil
2 oz. palm oil
3 oz. shea butter
4 oz. sunflower oil
13.2 oz. water
6.2 oz. lye
1 oz. sandalwood essential oil
2 oz. patchouli essential oil

Follow standard soap making instructions....

CASTILE SOAP

As a professional soap maker, the topic of castile soap is one of my personal pet peeves. It simply doesn't mean what it used to. Originally produced in Spain, it was made from pure olive oil only. Today, companies use the term to describe a soap that is made using just one type of oil. I've seen others have a variety of oils in the ingredient list and put the word "castile" on the label. Oh well, enough ranting. Here's a recipe for pure olive oil soap.

44 oz. olive oil
13.2 oz. water
5.6 oz. lye
(Optional) 3 oz. of your favorite essential oil.
If you decide to leave the batch unscented, add in 3 more ounces of water.
(keep in the mind that certain essential oils like clove and cinnamon can seize a batch of soap, especially when using 3 full ounces in a 44 ounces of oil base.)

Follow standard soap making instructions....

EASY OLIVE BAR

This recipe is sort of a spin on castile soap. Pure olive oil soap has a tendency to have a slimy feel to it. The addition of the castor oil seems to fix that, leaving you with just a super emollient soap.

2 oz. castor oil
42 oz. olive oil
13.5 oz. water
5.7 oz. lye
3 oz. of lavender or if you prefer to leave unscented, add in 3 more ounces of water and skip the essential oils.

Follow standard soap making instructions....

CALENDULA SOAP

The calendula flower has been used for centuries to calm irritated and sensitive skin. While the flower is abundantly easy to find, the essential oil is not. Occasionally, you may find a supplier with true calendula absolute but be prepared for the high price. For our soap, we're going to make a calendula tea and use it as our lye water.

Put approximately 20 (more than needed to allow for shrinkage) ounces of water in your tea kettle or favorite pot along with a handful of dried calendula petals on medium-high heat. When it reaches near the boiling point, remove from heat and allow to cool, stirring occasionally. Strain the flowers from your fresh batch of calendula tea and use (completely cooled) for your lye water. Using teas in your batch makes for an extra creamy soap.

27 oz. olive oil
10 oz. coconut oil
3 oz. cocoa butter
3 oz. palm oil
1 oz. shea butter
13.2 oz. calendula tea
6.1 oz. lye
2 oz. lavender essential oil
1 oz. palmarosa essential oil
4 teaspoons calendula petals

Follow standard soap making instructions....

CHEF'S COFFEE SOAP

Coffee soap is used primarily in the kitchen. It creates a chemical reaction that removes the smell of onion and garlic from your hands when washing with it. Just as we made tea for our calendula soap, now it's time to brew a pot of coffee. Brew a strong batch of coffee – at least as much as you'll need for your batch (13.2 ounces). Allow to completely cool and use as your lye water. Due to the addition of a full cup of coffee grounds to your oil batch, this recipe will make more than your mold can handle. Be prepared with an extra, single bar mold or throw the remainder of the batch away (never down the sink).

28 oz. olive oil
10 oz. vegetable shortening
6 oz. coconut oil
13.2 oz. water
5.8 oz. lye
2 oz. coffee fragrance oil
1 cup dark roasted coffee grounds

replace scent with water if you choose not to use coffee fragrance.

Follow standard soap making instructions....

LIME & AVOCADO BAR

The addition of avocado oil makes a super, gentle bar of soap. Sometimes you just have to splurge and use those luxury oils. The patchouli essential oil in this soap is just enough to make the scent of the lime and mandarin stronger, leaving very little patchouli smell. A touch of cocoa butter helps to make a harder bar of soap. Keep in mind that any recipes that contain cocoa butter may leave behind a slight chocolate scent. If you want to avoid this, look for deodorized cocoa butter when doing your shopping.

10 oz. avocado oil
3 oz. cocoa butter
12 oz. coconut oil
14 oz. olive oil
5 oz. palm oil
13.5 oz. water
6.3 oz. lye
2 oz. lime essential oil
1/2 oz. patchouli essential oil
1/2 oz. mandarin essential oil

Follow standard soap making instructions....

COCOA BUTTER SOAP

A high amount of cocoa butter not only makes for a hard bar of soap but leaves the skin feeling super soft. The only thing to keep in mind is that a lot of cocoa butter can sometimes make a recipe less sudsy than others. It does make for a good lather - just not the big, bubbly, frothy, kind. But when it feels this great, who cares? Cocoa butter is extracted directly from cocoa beans as a yellowish fatty acid.

4 oz. castor oil
12 oz. cocoa butter
8 oz. coconut oil
14 oz. olive oil
6 oz. soybean shortening
14 oz. water
6 oz. lye
2 oz. grapefruit essential oil
1/2 oz. lavender essential oil
1/2 oz. cedarwood essential oil

Follow standard soap making instructions....

LUXURY FACE BAR

This face bar soap recipe is for those with dry skin. Not only does the addition of shea butter help, but adding in the jojoba oil at trace leaves remnants of it behind, giving the skin more of a moisturizing boost. The blend of essential oils is: lavender, palmarosa and carrot. The lavender is mainly there to improve the scent of the carrot oil (not a favorite for everybody), but I happen to like it. Palmarosa and carrot essential oils are excellent for skin repair. If you are a fan, sneak in a little patchouli too. Your face will thank you.

5 oz. avocado oil
2 oz. castor oil
8 oz. coconut oil
17 oz. olive oil
6 oz. palm oil
2 oz. shea butter
4 oz. sunflower oil
13.5 oz water
6 oz. lye
1 oz. jojoba oil added at trace and blended in.
2 oz. lavender essential oil
.75 oz. palmarosa essential oil
.25 oz. carrot essential oil
1 Tablespoon calendula flowers
1/3 cup powdered oats

Follow standard soap making instructions....

SHEA & GINGER SOAP

Ginger is used primarily to warm and relax but it has also been used for centuries in Ayurvedic formulas for skin care. Research is showing that ginger also has anti-cellulite properties. The scent of ginger is known for helping with nausea and motion sickness. When blended with the uplifting smells of citrus, ginger is refreshing and invigorating.

4 oz. sweet almond oil
10 oz. coconut oil
15 oz. olive oil
5 oz. shea butter
10 oz. soybean shortening
13.5 oz. water
6.1 oz. lye
1 oz. bergamot essential oil
1/2 oz. ginger essential oil
1 oz. tangerine essential oil
1/2 oz. lemon essential oil
1 Tablespoon powdered ginger
1 teaspoon honey

Follow standard soap making instructions....

TOMATO SOAP

Yes, that's tomato *soap*, not soup. I've found several tomato soap recipes that suggest using whole pureed tomatoes as the lye water, supposedly because of their high water content. I tried it many years ago and found it to be a mess to work with and added more to the cleanup process. The lye mixed in with the tomatoes was not a friendly smell. In my opinion, using tomato paste added into your base oils was much more effective and made a nicer finished product. Tomatoes are used in many recipes by people who turn to a more organic approach to skincare but hardly anyone has heard about using the tomato for healthy skin. Tomatoes are said to shrink large pores, help with acne and rashes, and also have sunscreen benefits. I wouldn't go out sunbathing with just tomatoes on, though. If anything, it sounds terribly messy and a good way to attract insects to your lawn chair!

2 oz. cocoa butter
10 oz. coconut oil
25 oz. olive oil
4 oz. palm oil
3 oz. shea butter
13.5 oz. water
6.1 oz. lye
3 Tablespoons tomato paste (added at thin trace or before)
1 teaspoon dried basil leaves
3 oz. orange essential oil OR 2 oz. tomato leaf fragrance oil and 1 oz. water
Follow standard soap making instructions…

ICED LAVENDER SOAP

This blend of essential oils gives lavender a cool, exciting lift. I often use lavender mixed with tea tree for bug bites, especially mosquito bites. That is, whenever I've forgotten to use the mosquito soap or spray. Cornmint has a very similar scent to it as Peppermint. It is very potent and quite a bit of the essential oil is grown in the U.S.

2 oz. castor oil
10 oz. coconut oil
22 oz. olive oil
5 oz. palm oil
5 oz. safflower oil
13.5 oz. water
6.1 oz. lye
1.5 oz. lavender essential oil
1 oz. tea tree essential oil
1/2 oz. cornmint essential oil (may replace with peppermint)

Follow standard soap making instructions...

NOURISH THE SKIN LUXURY BAR

Okay, this recipe is a tad on the expensive side. So, remember that it is all right to be selfish now and then and keep the whole batch for yourself. Better not even tell your friends you made it or they'll be requesting it again and again. But the wide variety of skin loving oils in this bar of soap feels so good that you may not have any other choice than to brag about it.

4 oz. sweet almond oil
8 oz. coconut oil
2 oz. jojoba oil
18 oz. olive oil
6 oz. palm oil
4 oz. shea butter
2 oz. wheat germ oil
13.5 oz water
5.9 oz. lye
1 oz. palmarosa essential oil
1 oz. mandarin essential oil
1/2 oz. geranium essential oil
15 drops jasmine absolute (added at trace for maximum retention)

Follow standard soap making instructions...

MANGO BUTTER SOAP

I don't buy mango butter that often but when I do it is usually for a special batch I am going to make such as for Christmas presents or another event. Also, not a bad soap for those long winter months when your skin is feeling a little drier than usual.

3 oz. sweet almond oil
5 oz. canola oil
12 oz. coconut oil
5 oz. mango butter
14 oz. olive oil
5 oz. palm oil
13.5 oz. water
6.2 oz. lye
2 oz. orange essential oil
1 oz. litsea essential oil
OR
2 oz. mango fragrance oil plus 1 oz. extra water

Follow standard soap making instructions…

HEMP SOAP

This is another oil that I rarely use because it can have a short shelf life. But, it does impart a wonderful feeling on the skin. Sorry, all the "good" stuff is absent from hemp oil so you'll only get high on how great your body feels after a bath with this bar.

10 oz. coconut oil
10 oz. hemp oil
15 oz. olive oil
5 oz. palm oil
4 oz. safflower oil
14 oz. water
6.1 oz. lye
1 oz. clary sage essential oil
1 oz. lemongrass essential oil
1 oz. bergamot essential oil

Follow standard soap making instructions...

BEESWAX AND HONEY SOAP

Soap made with beeswax added makes a harder bar of soap with wonderful skin repair properties. It does, however, tend to accelerate trace so a little extra water is added to the recipe. Melt the beeswax in with your other oils and mix well when all have melted before adding your lye water solution. This way you know that all of the beeswax is incorporated if your batch moves along a little too quickly.

10 oz. coconut oil
12 oz. olive oil
20 oz. soybean shortening
2 oz. beeswax
14.5 oz water
5.9 oz. lye
1 Tablespoon honey
2 oz. sweet orange essential oil
1/4 oz. frankincense essential oil

Follow standard soap making instructions...

RECIPES MADE WITH ANIMAL FATS

Let me try to clarify something. There is nothing wrong with making soap using animal fats if that is what you want to do. The main reason I do not use them is personal preference and marketing. I mentioned them not being vegan-friendly. You see, our main retail store is located inside a wellness center where there are also yoga classes, acupuncture, massage, and vegetarian cooking classes. Considering the clientele of the building, going all-vegetable suits my business better. When I do make soap with animal fats in them, it is usually for our own use at home and most of the time we use lard.

All of the recipes found in this animal fats section contain no essential oils or fragrance oils. They are plain soap with a little extra water added. With my only offering a few recipes made with animal fats, I didn't want to confine you to my specific scent blends. This way, you can take any of the essential oil blends from other recipes in this book and use them in these recipes. If you do decide to add in essential oils or fragrance oils, remember to minus out about two ounces of the water because I have added more in, assuming it will be a non-scented soap.

100% LARD SOAP

Most soap makers will tell you that they like to add other oils to their lard soaps. Those that do make 100% lard soap usually use it as laundry soap because it makes such a super hard bar. But, I didn't want anyone thinking I wasn't willing to provide you with a one-oil soap without all those extra "fancy" oils included. Be warned, though. You have to cut this soap as soon as it is ready to come out of the mold. Don't wait a few days unless you want to bend the blade of your soap cutter. Did I mention it's a hard bar of soap?!

44 oz. pure lard
15 oz. water
5.8 oz. lye
(Remove 2 oz. water from recipe if you intend to add in essential oils)

Follow standard soap making instructions…

LARD PLUS SOAP RECIPE

Okay, you've had the chance to make just plain ole lard soap. Now let's add in some of those oils that will increase the soap's performance. Coconut for more lather and a touch of olive for moisturizing. Still a nice, hard bar of soap.

10 oz. coconut oil
4 oz. olive oil
30 oz. pure lard
15 oz. water
6.2 oz. lye
(Remove 2 oz. water from recipe if you intend to add in essential oils)

Follow standard soap making instructions…

BEEF TALLOW BAR

This is assuming you can actually find beef tallow. Sometimes, it is easier to look for all-beef shortening in the grocery store but that is also getting harder to find. Requires the same amount of lye to turn it into soap, whichever option you can find. After all, beef tallow and beef shortening are pretty much the exact same thing. One, you or someone else may have rendered and the other came from the shelf at the supermarket. The one in the store might give off less of an animal smell, though.

15 oz. coconut oil
9 oz. olive oil
20 oz. tallow or beef shortening
15 oz. water
6.45 oz. lye
(Remove 2 oz. water from recipe if you intend to add in essential oils)

Follow standard soap making instructions…

BEEF SHORTENING SOAP

This recipe requires a beef shortening that is a little easier to find in the grocery. It is a blend of beef shortening mixed with either cottonseed oil or soybean. It will say this on the container.

6 oz. castor oil
14 oz. coconut oil
24 oz. beef-vegetable shortening blend
15 oz. water
6.2 oz. lye
(Remove 2 oz. water from recipe if you intend to add in essential oils)

Follow standard soap making instructions...

HOW I MAKE SOAP
THE RTCP "MASTER BATCH" METHOD

First of all, I want to say that anything you could ever think of, someone else, somewhere else, has already been doing for a very long time. I don't claim to have invented these methods. I've taken bits of information that I've learned from others, combined them with my own experiences (sometimes mishaps that became blessings) and devised a method that worked best for me.

I made soap the same way for the first few years – melting each batch and waiting for it to cool, patiently waiting for the lye water to reach the same temperature as the cooling oils. When you have several soaps to be made, this process can take hours, even days to complete. One morning, I ran across an article in a small publication about a soap maker who had been making soap for several decades. He found the "temperature thing" totally unnecessary and a waste of time. Soon, I discovered other soap makers were discussing this method called RTCP: Room Temperature Cold Process.

To put it simply, RTCP is the act of premixing your oils and allowing them to cool to room temperature. Separately, the lye water is premixed, allowed to reach room temperature then simply mix the two batches together when its time for making soap. We are not going to learn RTCP. We are going to go a step beyond it.

The thought of having lye water lurking around unattended did not appeal to me. So, I decided to experiment with taking this method to another level. On the first day, I made what I now refer to as a "Master Batch". The Master Batch is made by premixing all of your soap making oils together ahead of time and letting them reach room temperature.

IMPORTANT FACT: One day I was reading Amazon reviews of the first edition of this book and I came across a less than favorable review. The reader's main complaint was that my entire book was about premixing a big master batch of lye. No. I'll say it again – no. Obviously, the woman did not read the book. She must have just skimmed it. In *one* place I mentioned that some soap makers do this but I do not and that the Master Batch method is all about premixing your carrier oils – NOT lye!

The Master Batch recipe will take you through all of the basic recipes in the second recipe section of this book. They are the soaps that are the closest to what we sell in our own soap making business. This large master batch will give you enough base to make five full loaves of soap; each loaf creating twelve, four ounce bars when fully cured. Also, this section of the book is geared more towards economical soap making. Many of the recipes in the first section of the book used luxury oils and ingredients. Here, we will use oils that are affordable and can often be found in your grocery store or restaurant supply store: shortening, olive oil, and coconut oil. Just great soap from simple ingredients that you, your family, and potential customers will love.

Additional equipment for the Master Batch Recipe -

Empty, clean, five gallon bucket
Large canning pot for melting (23 quarts or more)

Master Batch Recipe:

7 lbs. 8 ounces Vegetable Shortening*
3 lbs. 2 ounces Coconut Oil
3 lbs. 2 ounces Olive Oil

*vegetable shortening varies in different parts of the United States. Some regions have a partial cottonseed blend which shouldn't affect your soap at all. Crisco-type shortening is a good alternative. Just be sure to read the labels carefully when doing your shopping - many shortenings contain beef fat or partial beef fat. This master batch recipe calls for all-vegetable shortening.

Measure Olive Oil into your empty five gallon bucket and set aside. Now measure your vegetable shortening and coconut oil into your large canning pot and melt on the stovetop on medium-low. When fully melted, carefully pour the contents into your waiting bucket of olive oil. (It's best to place the bucket of olive oil on the floor to avoid any mishaps). Now, stir with your stick blender until fully mixed. I use an electric drill with a paint stirring attachment for blending the master batch. As the batch cools, repeat the stirring process whenever you get the chance and allow to cool overnight. The next day, give it a final, vigorous blending until the mixture looks fully incorporated. The final master batch will have a runny, pudding-like quality to it. You now have five full batches of soaping oils ready to be measured out individually and turned into soap. Over time you will recognize if your Master Batch needs a good mixing before beginning a day of soaping.

With these recipes, each time you begin making soap you will measure out 2 lbs. 12 ounces of master batch.
Master Soap Recipe:
2 lbs. 12 ounces master batch
13.5 ounces water
6.2 ounces lye

Here is where the time-saving tips come into play - when making soap, I don't wait for anything to cool, wait for a certain time to color my batch or try to figure out when to scent the batch. Using the same safety guidelines listed in the Standard Soap Making Instructions (goggles, gloves, respect for the lye, etc.) here is the way I normally make soap.

STEP ONE - Measure 2 lbs. 12 ounces of master batch into a 3 gallon bucket.

STEP TWO - Weigh 13.5 ounces of water into my lye pitcher then slowly add the 6.2 ounces of lye and stir until dissolved.

STEP THREE - Add colorant (usually oxides) into master batch and stir with stick blender until fully colored.

STEP FOUR - Add any botanicals / additives the recipe calls for.

STEP FIVE - Weigh and measure essential oils and add to the master batch, stirring again.

STEP SIX - Slowly pour the hot lye water into the 3 gallon bucket of colored and scented master batch and begin mixing with stick blender. Trace usually takes approximately five to ten minutes before it's ready to pour into the molds.

Basically, what I have done is streamlined every step that was time-consuming, turning the operation into a smooth day of batch-after-batch soap making. Pretty easy, huh?

IMPORTANT
DO NOT skip over anything that is a safety precaution! Wear your goggles and gloves, remember that lye is corrosive and don't forget to hold your face away from the pan while mixing. Remember to keep your stick blender immersed in the soap you are blending and don't splash around. Don't forget - you add lye to water, you do NOT add water to lye. (The snow falls on the lake, remember?) Your eyesight and the safety of your children and your pets are more important than any batch of soap. If you remain aware of what you are doing and do it with thought, you'll be fine. Simply pay attention to what you're doing and it will be as easy as baking a cake.

MASTER BATCH SOAP RECIPES

Now we are ready to tackle a variety of recipes using the same "base" of oils that we have called the "Master Batch". Despite their simplicity, the recipes that follow are some really great soaps! Each of these recipes was poured into wooden molds with inside measurements that were 14.5 inches long, 3.5 inches deep and 3 inches wide.

If you find that you like some of the recipes found here but do not want to use the Master Batch method, on the bottom of this page is the recipe you will use if you choose to melt each batch from scratch, just like you did in the first section of this book. You may use the recipe in place of any of the following recipes in this Master Batch section of the book where it calls for 2 lbs, 12 ounces of master batch. For standard soap making, where you melt all oils then keep a close eye on oil and lye water temperature, here is that recipe:

24 oz. vegetable shortening
10 oz. coconut oil
10 oz. olive oil

Okay, let's get started soaping....

GRAPEFRUIT ORANGE SOAP

This bar is great for anyone that loves citrus scents. This particular soap takes a little longer to trace and the addition of calendula petals makes pretty yellow flecks throughout the soap. Soaps with all citrus oils have a tendency to "lock in" the fragrance when cured. Meaning, the bar doesn't seem to smell very strong but will when you get the soap wet in the bath or shower. If you'd like to anchor the scent a little more, replace 1/2 ounce of the sweet orange essential oil with patchouli essential oil.

2 lbs. 12 oz. master batch
13.5 oz. water
6.2 oz. lye
1 oz. pink grapefruit essential oil
1 oz. sweet orange essential oil
1 oz. 5-fold orange essential oil
3 tablespoons calendula petals
1/16 teaspoon yellow oxide colorant

Follow soap making instructions....

SUNSHINE SOAP

The reason I call this bar "sunshine" is the fact that it is a great scent to wake up with. The peppermint helps to wake you up in the morning while the citrus oils bring about a cheerful mood to start the day with.

2 lbs. 12 oz. master batch
13.5 oz. water
6.2 oz. lye
1 oz. pink grapefruit essential oil
1.5 oz. sweet orange essential oil
1/2 oz. peppermint essential oil
1 teaspoon peppermint leaves
1/16 teaspoon fluorescent yellow pigment

Follow soap making instructions…

LEMONGRASS & CLARY SAGE SOAP

Men and women both love this soap. It seems to be a favorite all year long and holds its scent quite well. The scent of lemongrass is said to promote psychic awareness and is widely used in perfumery. Clary sage oil is not to be confused with regular cooking sage. Clary Sage is known for having properties that mimic the female hormone while lemongrass is uplifting to the spirits. When the two are mixed together, it creates a blend that is said to be good for depression, PMS and menopause. Men buy it for the great smell. Women like it for the properties and the great scent.

2 lbs. 12 oz. master batch
13.5 oz. water
6.2 oz. lye
2 oz. lemongrass essential oil
1 oz. clary sage essential oil
1 teaspoon lemongrass herb (cut & sifted)
1/8 teaspoon yellow oxide colorant

Follow soap making instructions…

TEA TREE LIME SOAP

Tea tree makes a wonderful bar of soap for acne and athlete's foot. A favorite among men and teenagers, this is a bar that sells well to people who have a good knowledge of essential oils and their benefits. I've always found tea tree to have a pleasant smell but many find it to be too strong. The addition of lime essential oil brings a fun scent to the medicinal smell of tea tree.

2 lbs. 12 oz. master batch
13.5 oz. water
6.2 oz. lye
2 oz. tea tree essential oil
1 oz. lime essential oil
1/16 teaspoon green oxide colorant
1/16 teaspoon titanium dioxide (white pigment)

Follow soap making instructions…

TANGERINE & HONEY SOAP

This recipe smells really wonderful in the shower but you can't let it sit too long before cutting it into bars. Something about all the citrus in the recipe makes the loaf become really hard after twenty-four hours. If you find that you would like to anchor the tangerine scent a little more, try replacing half of the sweet orange essential oil with patchouli.

2 lbs. 12 oz. master batch
13.5 oz. water
6.2 oz. lye
2 oz. tangerine essential oil
1 oz. sweet orange essential oil
1/4 teaspoon yellow oxide
1/4 teaspoon red oxide
1 teaspoon powdered or regular honey

Follow soap making instructions...

LAVENDER SOAP

Lavender soap is one of the first things that come to mind when people think about handmade soap. Few people realize how strong essential oils actually are. It takes an acre of lavender plants to get approximately twelve pounds of lavender essential oil. Best known for its relaxation qualities, lavender essential oil is the first thing we reach for in our household when it comes to burns and bug bites.

2 lbs. 12 oz. master batch
13.5 oz. water
6.2 oz. lye
3 oz. lavender essential oil
2 teaspoons lavender buds

Follow soap making instructions....

LAVENDER LIME SOAP

Adding a splash of lime essential oil to lavender soap turns it into a really fun soap. As a matter of fact, it's the way we usually get men to try lavender. Women who like citrus smells love it too. Lime oil has properties that are similar to lemon. It is said to work well as an astringent and a deodorant.

2 lbs. 12 oz. master batch
13.5 oz. water
6.2 oz. lye
2 oz. lavender essential oil
1 oz. lime essential oil
1/8 teaspoon green oxide colorant

Follow soap making instructions…

LAVENDER PATCHOULI SOAP

These two essential oils work wonderfully together. The patchouli makes the scent of lavender stronger while adding an earthy undertone at the same time. Since our company makes so many types of lavender soap, I like to color this one pale brown to remind people about the addition of the patchouli. Usually, frequent customers go hunting for it by looking for the familiar color.

2 lbs. 12 oz. master batch
13.5 oz. water
6.2 oz. lye
2 oz. lavender essential oil
1 oz. patchouli essential oil
1/16 teaspoon brown oxide colorant
2 teaspoons lavender buds

Follow soap making instructions…

LAVENDER ROSEMARY SOAP

Out of all the lavender soaps our company has made over the years, this one outsells the others. Usually, I create this soap with a bright purple swirl throughout the cream colored soap. You can achieve this by adding the violet oxide (listed below) and placing it in a small container that is still large enough to accommodate your stick blender. Add a teaspoon of water to dampen the oxide and go about your regular soap making. At trace, pour around a half a cup of soap into the container you set aside and stick blend until purple. Pour the purple into your mold first, then, the rest of your uncolored batch. For more detailed instructions, refer to the front of the book under the "swirling" section.

2 lbs. 12 oz. master batch
13.5 oz. water
6.2 oz. lye
2 oz. lavender essential oil
1 oz. rosemary essential oil
1/2 teaspoon violet oxide colorant (added separately, see above)
2 teaspoons lavender buds

Follow soap making instructions....

LAVENDER SPEARMINT SOAP

Spearmint is definitely the first thing you smell in this soap. However, the lavender gives it a light, carefree scent that mellows out the mint. If you'd rather not color this batch violet or lavender, try experimenting with different shades of green to bring out the word "mint" in the name.

2 lbs. 12 oz. master batch
13.5 oz. water
6.2 oz. lye
2 oz. lavender essential oil
1 oz. spearmint essential oil
1 teaspoon violet oxide colorant
2 teaspoons lavender buds

Follow soap making instructions....

LAVENDER ORANGE SOAP

Children and adults both like this soap. Personally, I think it smells like Fruit Loops when it gets wet. I like to make this soap in a pale orange color, using mainly yellow with a little bit of red. If you would like a creamier looking shade of orange, try adding a touch of white to the formula.

2 lbs. 12 oz. master batch
13.5 oz. water
6.2 oz. lye
2 oz. lavender essential oil
1 oz. 5-fold orange essential oil
1/4 teaspoon yellow oxide colorant
1/8 teaspoon red oxide
2 teaspoons lavender buds

Follow soap making instructions....

GARDEN GATE SOAP

This is one of my favorite soaps. It has been a best seller in our company for over ten years. The large amount of herbs in the recipe act as a wonderful exfoliant and the addition of honey not only feels great on the skin, but also turns the base a pale, golden color. Spearmint is definitely the first thing your nose detects but customers have to keep sniffing to figure out the rest of the blend. This soap is named as a nod to the book and movie *Practical Magic* (the original inspiration for the company) where it is mentioned that you should plant lavender for luck and keep rosemary by your garden gate.

2 lbs. 12 oz. master batch
13.5 oz. water
6.2 oz. lye
2 oz. lavender essential oil
3/4 oz. spearmint essential oil
1/4 oz. peppermint essential oil
3 teaspoons lavender buds
1/2 teaspoon powdered rosemary
1 teaspoon peppermint leaves
1 teaspoon powdered or regular honey

Follow soap making instructions....

PEPPERMINT SOAP

This one is very tingly if you use too much peppermint so don't go over the recommended two ounces essential oil per batch. Not recommended for people with super-sensitive skin. Allow to fully cure before using. Can be too tingly on "sensitive" areas, if you know what I mean. Peppermint is said to be great for tension headaches. Also, this soap is excellent in the summer for people who jog or work outdoors in the heat. It has a "cooling" action in the shower.

2 lbs. 12 oz. master batch
13.5 oz. water
6.2 oz. lye
2 oz. peppermint essential oil
1 oz. extra water (to make up for the missing ounce of essential oil)
1 teaspoon spearmint leaves
2 teaspoons peppermint leaves

Follow soap making instructions....

GARDENER'S SOAP

Working in the garden requires a little extra cleaning action. The cornmeal in the recipe helps to scrub away dirt. Essential oil of orange is good for cutting dirt and grease while the spearmint and eucalyptus essential oils bring a fresh smell to hands that have been digging in the ground. A great way to sell this soap as a gift is to take natural twine and tie the bar to the palm of a pair of gardener's gloves.

2 lbs. 12 oz. master batch
13.5 oz. water
6.2 oz. lye
2 oz. sweet orange essential oil
1/2 oz. spearmint essential oil
1/2 oz. eucalyptus essential oil
4 teaspoons yellow cornmeal
1 teaspoon pumice or oatmeal

Follow soap making instructions....

ROSEMARY SOAP

The name speaks for itself. Rosemary is an excellent deodorizing soap. It has a scent that is fresh, camphorous and woodsy, all at the same time. In aromatherapy, it is supposed to bring clarity of mind, help with memory loss and ease nervous tension. If you would like to color this soap naturally, leave out the green oxide and increase the amount of powdered rosemary to six teaspoons. Makes an earthy, greenish, tan color.

2 lbs. 12 oz. master batch
13.5 oz. water
6.2 oz. lye
3 oz. rosemary essential oil
2 teaspoons powdered rosemary
Sprinkle of green oxide colorant

Follow soap making instructions....

EUCALYPTUS SOAP

Like the tangerine soap, eucalyptus soap is another one that you want to cut into bars as soon as possible. When allowed to sit around too long, the edges seem to become brittle. On the plus side, something about the eucalyptus oil seems to boost the lather in the soap. Wonderful for bathing when you have a cold or the flu.

2 lbs. 12 oz. master batch
13.5 oz. water
6.2 oz. lye
3 oz. eucalyptus essential oil
1/4 teaspoon blue oxide
(optional) teaspoon crushed eucalyptus leaves

Follow soap making instructions....

PATCHOULI SOAP

Fans of the Sixties love this soap. It's making a comeback with the new, urban hippie style that is spreading across America. This essential oil is earthy, exotic and grounding. I added a touch of powdered clove to give it dark flecks and it seems to add something extra to the scent. Feel free to leave out the clove if you prefer. It is also beautiful when you add just a hint of red oxide to the brown, giving it the color of red clay. Experiment, make it your own.

2 lbs. 12 oz. master batch
13.5 oz. water
6.2 oz. lye
3 oz. patchouli essential oil
1/2 teaspoon brown oxide colorant
1 teaspoon powdered clove

Follow soap making instructions....

PATCHOULI MINT SOAP

The heavy, earthy smell of the patchouli mixed with the fresh scent of spearmint turns into a delightful scent you wouldn't normally expect. Even people who don't like patchouli seem to favor this one.

2 lbs. 12 oz. master batch
13.5 oz. water
6.2 oz. lye
2 oz. patchouli essential oil
1 oz. spearmint essential oil
1/8 teaspoon brown oxide colorant
1 teaspoon spearmint leaves

Follow soap making instructions....

SPICED TEA SOAP

Spicy, as the name suggests, but also light enough to please those people who don't normally choose "earthy" scents in their soap. The cinnamon essential oil, along with the cinnamon and clove herbs in this recipe, can accelerate trace – it is perfectly acceptable to add another ounce or two of water to this recipe if you experience problems.

2 lbs. 12 oz. master batch
13.5 oz. water
6.2 oz. lye
3 oz. sweet orange essential oil
12 drops cinnamon leaf essential oil
1 teaspoon powdered clove
1 teaspoon powdered cinnamon
1 teaspoon powdered ginger
2 teaspoons calendula petals

Follow soap making instructions....

HOLIDAY POMANDER SPICE SOAP

During Victorian times it was popular to make pomanders to scent the room, especially at Christmas time. Normally, one would take an orange, puncture it with holes and fill the holes with whole cloves. Sometimes, it was then rolled in cinnamon and placed on a dish to scent the room. When dried, some used pomanders as ornaments for the holiday tree. Like the spice tea soap, some of the ingredients speed up trace. Feel free to use a bit more water if you run into problems. The best solution is to work quickly and get your traced batch into your mold.

2 lbs. 12 oz. master batch
13.5 oz. water
6.2 oz. lye
1 oz. patchouli essential oil
2 oz. sweet orange essential oil
12 drops cinnamon leaf essential oil
1/2 teaspoon brown oxide colorant
1 teaspoon powdered clove
1 teaspoon powdered cinnamon

Follow soap making instructions....

CLOVE SOAP

Clove essential oil speeds up trace faster than any other essential oil that I have soaped with before. Its scent is also strong and requires less essential oil than other recipes. Work quickly. You will also notice that this recipe calls for more water. This aids in slowing down trace.

2 lbs. 12 oz. master batch
15 oz. water
6.2 oz. lye
1/2 oz. clove bud essential oil
2.5 oz. extra water
2 teaspoons powdered clove

Follow soap making instructions...

MOSQUITO SOAP

There are many essential oils that fight off mosquitoes and ticks. Many years ago, a friend actually asked me to come up with something that would help her son who liked to go camping but always returned home covered in mosquito bites and ticks. I created a spray using the essential oil formula below (blended in spring water and vodka). Then I wondered how it would perform in soap. It worked like a charm. We use the soap when we go camping, even washing our hair with it. Citronella is the most widely known and the most recognizable when it comes to the scent. Mixing citronella with other oils that have similar properties creates an effective bug-fighting soap with a more appealing scent. Lemon eucalyptus was reported by the CDC to be the best, natural alternative to Deet.

2 lbs. 12 oz. master batch
13.5 oz. water
6.2 oz. lye
1 oz. citronella essential oil
1 oz. lemon eucalyptus essential oil
1/2 oz. cedarwood essential oil
1/2 oz. lavender essential oil
1/4 teaspoon yellow oxide colorant

Follow soap making instructions....

LICORICE SOAP

Real licorice root doesn't smell like licorice candy at all. The candy is actually flavored with anise essential oil, the smell that everyone associates with the word "licorice". At one time, we called this soap "Bewitched" because it looked very mysterious, made in white with a black swirl. But, not many people cared for the name, so we changed it to Licorice soap. If you want to make a black swirl in the soap, follow the instructions for coloring in the swirling section of this book and use black oxide. This soap traces slowly. You have plenty of time to dump your black soap into the middle of your soap pot if you are going for a marbled effect.

2 lbs. 12 oz. master batch
13.5 oz. water
6.2 oz. lye
2 oz. lavender essential oil
1 oz. anise essential oil

Follow soap making instructions....

GOATS MILK WITH YLANG-YLANG SOAP

I love the smell of ylang-ylang. It comes in several grades but I've always found ylang-ylang II to be my favorite. It is an exotic, flowery scent that tends to take over other essential oils. Keep this in mind if you want to start creating some essential oil blends that include ylang-ylang – a little goes a long way. It is widely used in perfumery and expensive body care products. Ylang-ylang is also said to be an aphrodisiac. Women wear it to attract men.

2 lbs. 12 oz. master batch
13.5 oz. water
6.2 oz. lye
2 oz. ylang-ylang essential oil
1 oz. patchouli essential oil
2 teaspoons powdered goat's milk

Follow soap making instructions....

OATMEAL MILK & HONEY SOAP

Our version really doesn't have a fragrance but it feels wonderful on the skin. Personally, I think it smells like pound cake --- everyone else says, "I don't smell anything". Many of our customers with eczema swear by this soap. For a more interesting and textured look, sprinkle whole oats onto the top of the soap right after pouring into the mold.

2 lbs. 12 oz. master batch
13.5 oz. water
6.2 oz. lye
3 oz. cow's milk
4 teaspoons powdered oatmeal
2 teaspoons powdered or regular honey

Follow soap making instructions....

AN OVERVIEW OF ESSENTIAL OILS

One of the greatest treats in soap making is experimenting with combinations of essential oils. Unlike fragrance oils, which are usually chemically manufactured scents, essential oils are very potent. Each oil, like the plants they are derived from, is different in their basic makeup which is why there is such a difference in price among the oils. Essential oils can begin (at wholesale pricing) in the neighborhood of $12 per pound all the way up to $1300 per pound (and more).

Many people have asked whether the aromatherapy benefits survive the soap making process. To my knowledge, as of this writing, that research has not been done. Chemically, many of them most likely do, to a degree. I do believe the emotional benefits of the oils come through in soap. Smelling them activates the olfactory system and can bring about a shift in emotions. Mints have the ability to wake you up, Citrus oils are cheering, Lavender seems to relax you, etc.

You will have to decide for yourself which oils you would like to use according to their safety precautions. Using essential oils in soap is definitely a manner of "diluting" an oil. Furthermore, the soap is rinsed off in the bath or shower -- unlike a massage where the essential oils are rubbed into the skin via a carrier oil and left on the skin until the next bath time.

The essential oil list on the following pages is meant for

information purposes regarding the way essential oils are currently being used. If you have any concerns, feel free to consult a physician before using a specific oil. It is probably always a good idea to listen to the advice of the pregnancy precautions.

Anise – (pimpinella anisum)

Sweet, licorice-like scent often used during the hunting season to mask the human scent. Also applied to bait to attract fish. Cheering, euphoric, energizing, sense enhancing, antibacterical, coughs, deodorant, menopause. Parts used: seed pod. Dilute well before use. Do not use during pregnancy.

Bergamot – (citrus bergamia)

Citrusy, fresh, woodsy scent. Cheering, concentration, aggression, confidence, grief, nervous tension and stress. Said to help with the stress of Parkinson's Disease and PMS moodiness. Good for withdrawals. Parts used: peel of fruit. Phototoxic. Do not expose applied area of skin to direct sunlight or tanning bed for 24 hours.

Cedarwood – (cedrus atlantica)

Dry, sweet, woodsy balsamic scent. Balancing, grounding and strengthening. Often used to promote self-control and to balance spirituality. Possible uses: acne, dry hair, rheumatism, oily skin, immunity booster. Parts used: wood. Avoid during pregnancy. May irritate extra sensitive skin.

Cinnamon Leaf – (cinnamomum zeylancium)

Hot, spicy scent — richer in aroma than ground cinnamon. Invigorating, refreshing, warming, aphrodisiac properties. Often used by those with low blood pressure. Good for exhaustion & fatigue. Antifungal. Parts used: leaf. Avoid if you have high blood pressure. Dilute well before use.

Citronella–(cymbopogon nardus)

Slightly fruity, fresh, lemony scent. An oil that is known to be refreshing, stimulating, soothing & vitalizing. Most popular for being a powerful insect repellent. Antiseptic properties, good when you have a cold. Parts used: grass. Avoid during pregnancy.

Clary Sage – (salvia sclarea)

Earthy, herbaceous & slightly fruity scent. Known as the "woman's oil." Good for use as an antidepressant, for PMS and Menopause. Also good for fatigue, fear & stress. Is often used to help promote vivid dreaming. Parts used: flowering tops, herb. Avoid with a history of breast or ovarian cysts or estrogen-dependent cancer. Do not overuse while drinking alcohol.

Clove Bud – (eugenia caryophyllata)

Spicy, warming, rich but slightly bitter scent. Possible uses: memory loss, stimulating, energizing, warming. Also known for use as an antiseptic, for sprains, strains and is often used (in part) by dentists for toothache. Parts used: flower buds. A possible mucous membrane irritant. Not to be used by alcoholics or those with prostate cancer.

Eucalyptus – (eucalyptus globulus)

Clean, fresh, medicinal scent. A balancing, cooling & stimulating oil often used with colds, coughs, muscular fatigue & sinusitis. Also helpful when you have bronchitis, the flu or slight fever. Parts used: leaves & twigs. Avoid with a history of epilepsy or if you are using homeopathic remedies. Do NOT take internally — toxic.

Fir Needle – (Abies alba)

Woody, earthy, fresh scent. Known for stimulating circulation. Often used for muscle pain, arthritis & rheumatism as well as elevating the emotions and helping with stress. Parts used: leaves (needles), twigs. Dilute well before use.

Frankincense – (Boswellia carterii)

Spicy, woody, fruity & fresh smell. For the mind, frankincense is often used for anxiety, exhaustion and for focus. Reported to help with scars and wrinkles. Has been used in history for blessing and consecration. Parts used: resin. Avoid during pregnancy. Regarded as generally safe.

Geranium – (Pelargonium graveolens)

Floral but sweet smell with fruity undertones. Often used for nerves, stress and for relaxed, intense focus (such as self-hypnosis). Has been known to calm those who suffer from Alzheimer's and Muscular Dystrophy. Parts used: flowers, leaves, stalks. Avoid if a history of estrogen-dependent cancer or hypoglycemia.

Ginger – (Zingiber officinale)

Smoky, spicy, woody scent. For the mind, used for memory loss and to anchor the emotions. Good for nausea, motion sickness, aches & sprains and the nausea associated with migraine headaches. Parts used: roots (stems). May irritate extra-sensitive skin. Dilute well before use.

Jasmine Absolute – (Jasminum officinalis)

Exotic, floral, rich, sweet scent. Used often in the perfume industry. Has relaxing, sedative properties and is said to be an aphrodisiac. Also good as an antidepressant, for PMS & Menopause. Parts used: flowers. Avoid during pregnancy. Extended use has narcotic-like properties.

Juniper Berry – (juniperus communis)

Crisp, sweet & herbaceous with a fruity note. Often used for gout, jet lag and hangovers as well as for memory loss, clearing the mind and exhaustion. Said to have detoxifying and toning properties. Parts used: berries. Avoid during pregnancy. Avoid if a history of kidney disease or high blood pressure.

Lavender – (lavandula officinalis)

Floral, fresh, light, herbaceous scent. Is said to bring about love and peace. Good for insect bites, to calm the nerves, help with sleeping — soothing & relaxing. Also good for burns, bruises, itching and headaches. Parts used: flowering tops. Avoid during first trimester of pregnancy.

Lemon – (citrus limonum)

Rich, fresh smell similar to fresh lemon rinds. Used to uplift the spirits as it is balancing, cheering and refreshing. Often used to reduce warts, for fainting and hayfever. Good ingredient in cleaning and dish washing. Parts used: peel of fruit. Phototoxic. Do not expose applied area of skin to direct sunlight or tanning bed for 24 hours.

Lemon Eucalyptus – (eucalyptus citriodora)

Sweet, lemony smell with a woody note. Known to be calming and purifying. Reported by the CDC to be a good, natural substitution for DEET in combating mosquitoes. Contains some of the same properties as regular eucalyptus. Parts used: leaves, twigs. Dilute before use.

Lemongrass – (cymbopogon citratus)

Fresh, lemony, grassy scent. For the mind, used for irritability, mental fatigue, stress & nervous exhaustion. Often used as a mild insect repellent, for light cases of athlete's foot and reported to be good for cellulite. Parts used: grass, leaves. Avoid during pregnancy or a history of high blood pressure.

Lime – (citrus aurantifolia)

Green, fresh, citrusy, sweet scent. Stimulating, uplifting & cheering, lime is known for helping raise the spirits and makes a good antidepressant. Good for skin toning as an astringent and is said to help with dandruff. Parts used: peel of fruit. Mildly phototoxic. Try to avoid direct exposure to sunlight where lime has been used on the skin.

Litsea – (litsea cubeba)

Also known as May Chang. Litsea is an evergreen tree or shrub that grows in places like China, Indonesia, and Thailand. In chemical composition, it is very similar to lemon verbena and can be used as an affordable replacement to the more expensive verbena oil. Deep, lemony scent but more complex than lemon oil. Is said to be helpful in treating acne and oily skin as well as muscular aches and chills. Parts used: fruit. Avoid during pregnancy.

Palmarosa – (cymbopogon martini)

A floral, grassy, rose-like scent. Good for creativity, aggression & anxiety. Said to work quite well for wrinkles, dermatitis, hair loss & PMS symptoms. Associated with healing and love. Parts used: whole plant. Avoid with a history of high blood pressure.

Patchouli – (pogostemon cablin)

Rich, earthy, woody aroma. Known as a general aphrodisiac. Good for relaxation as well as concentration. Said to be good for wrinkles, acne, dandruff and athlete's foot. Best known as the incense commonly used in the 1960's. Parts used: leaves. Generally regarded as safe. Do not take internally.

Peppermint – (mentha piperita)

Minty, strong peppermint candy smell. Cooling, refreshing, revitalizing and stimulating. Is good for headaches, nausea & jet lag. Mixed in base oils or lotions, is good for muscular aches and rheumatoid arthritis. Parts used: whole plant

Avoid during pregnancy or a history of high blood pressure. Use in small amounts. Avoid contact with eyes.

Pink Grapefruit – (citrus paradisi)

Citrusy scent, similar to a grapefruit rind. A good uplifting oil - good for concentration and to promote happy thoughts. Reported to be good for migraines, hangovers, PMS symptoms & hair loss as well as being antibacterial. Parts used: peel of fruit. Phototoxic. Avoid contact with the sun or tanning beds after using oil on skin.

Rosemary – (rosmarinus officinalis)

Sweet, fresh, herb-like, medicinal scent. Good for grief and fatigue as well as clearing out the mind. Often used as an antiviral, a decongestant and for muscular aches. Also known as an immunity stimulant. Parts used: leaves. Avoid during pregnancy or a history of high blood pressure or epilepsy.

Rosewood – (aniba rosaeodora)

Sweet, woody and fruity with a floral scent. Good for mild cases of depression and clearing out confusion. Often used for headaches, PMS, scars, sensitive skin and stretch marks. Parts used: wood, twigs. Generally regarded as safe. Do not take internally.

Sandalwood – (santalum album)

Woodsy, balsamic, deep perfume-like scent. Used to center the thoughts and also used in meditation and as an aphrodisiac. Known for being used for wrinkles, chapped skin, dry hair and dandruff. Parts used: wood. Do not take internally.

Spearmint – (mentha spicata)

Fresh, minty, sweet smell — less potent than peppermint. Often used for sniffing during times of morning sickness. Also good for stimulating and reviving as well as asthma, headache and nausea. Parts used: leaves. Use in small amounts. Large amounts may irritate mucous membranes.

Sweet Orange – (citrus sinensis)

Citrusy, sweet, strong scent like orange peels. Good antidepressant and uplifting oil. Has been used for drug withdrawal symptoms, stress and for its slight sedative properties. Often associated with joy, luck and money. Parts used: peel of fruit. Avoid use in sun. May irritate sensitive skin if not diluted properly.

Tangerine – (citrus reticulata)

Bright, deep citrusy smell like tangerine peels. Relaxing, cheering & soothing. Astringent, Antiseptic, Antispasmodic, Antidepressant. Parts used: peel of fruit. Avoid use in sun. May irritate sensitive skin if not diluted properly.

Tea Tree – (melaleuca alternifolia)

An herbaceous, green, earthy scent — slightly medicinal. The scent has cleansing and cooling properties. Has been used for centuries for burns, bug bites, scrapes and cuts. Also good for athlete's foot, blisters, boils and sunburns.

Parts used: leaves, twigs. Do not take internally. Can be used neat (undiluted) in small amounts on many people. Test patch first.

Ylang-Ylang – (cananga odorata)

Floral, slightly fruity, delicate, perfume-like scent. Promotes euphoria, relaxation and is often thought of as an aphrodisiac. Lowers blood pressure. Good for its sedative properties and for shock. Parts used: flowers. Avoid if a history of apnea or low blood pressure.

SELLING, PACKAGING AND LABELING
YOUR SOAPS

HOW TO DISPLAY YOUR SOAP AT A SHOW OR CRAFT FAIR

We have used baskets to display our soaps for years. Mainly because baskets create the illusion that there is more soap than you actually have. When soaps are stacked on top of each other or in a straight line from front to back, it creates the visual of a single product - the eyes only see the first bar. But when the soaps are haphazardly arranged inside a small basket, the presentation is rustic and inviting. It lures customers to actually pick up the soap and smell it. The soap spreading out in all directions gives the illusion of quantity. Baskets are easy to find. Just look in local dollar stores, especially around the holidays. We know one soap maker that uses HUGE baskets - actually they are wicker laundry baskets, completely filled with bars of soap. For her, it makes for a better presentation because she only makes about eight varieties of handmade soap. So, this large quantity of only eight types is a very impressive display. It tells her customers, "I make soap, lots of soap and there's plenty more where that came from."

SETTING UP A FLEA MARKET DISPLAY

Setting up an entire soap display for a flea market or craft fair doesn't have to be difficult. We do it with nothing more than a six foot table, two wooden boards, some mini milk crates and two pieces of cloth. We set up a booth at the Nashville Fairgrounds flea market one weekend a month for almost three years before opening our store. We didn't use baskets for display at the market but we brought so MUCH soap with us that it still made for a good presentation.

Our market setup was a 10 x 10 booth space. We purposely chose to inset the six-foot table about two feet from the back of the booth space. This way, customers could step into the booth space without being rushed in the aisle by other shoppers and we could stand behind the table, also out of their way and be ready to answer their questions. The extra space behind the table left enough room for two, folding, camping chairs (we would take turns sitting) and the stair-step effect on the table gave lots of room behind (and under) it for - the cash box, shopping bags, lunch, credit card slips, etc.

How to create the stair-step effect: Set up your table. First, cover the table with your first table cloth. To create two tiers, you will need: 2, six foot long wooden boards as wide as -- the milk crates you're going to buy.

Set up three milk crates in the middle of the table, one at each end and one in the center. Behind those crates, you will need six milk crates set up the same way but stacked two-high. These are mini milk crates, mind you, not the huge ones that are actually for delivering milk. They are also found in many dollar stores but you can also buy them in stores like Office Depot for around $2.00 each. Stores such as the DOLLAR TREE sometimes carry them for $1.00. Next, place the boards across the milk crates to create your shelving. Now, take the second table cloth and drape it over your makeshift staircase. By placing the crates in the middle and back of the table, the table itself becomes a third (or bottom) step in your display.

If you want to make an L-shape, set up a four foot table beside your six foot running in the opposite direction. In the beginning, we used burlap to cover the shelving and a dark green tablecloth for the table. Later on, we began using all solid green and liked it much better. If you choose fabrics that are 100% polyester, you will find you don't have to do a lot of ironing before a show. Just wash and carefully fold or roll the fabric. Of course, you want to pick a fabric color that reflects the theme of your company. We chose hunter green because it was earthy as well as eye catching. Also, earth tones and greens give off a more natural appeal to showcase natural products.

MAKING SALES AT YOUR MARKET EVENT

When you're first starting out, word of mouth is the very best sales tool. But there are other ways to reach new customers, people that you don't already know. Festivals and flea markets are a great way to do this. Usually, the booth rental is affordable and you can get your face (and your product) out in front of the public. Besides your soaps, make sure to take plenty of business cards with you. Give them not only to the customers that purchased soap, but also to the ones that seemed interested but didn't make a purchase.

When you do a festival or flea market, be sure to take plenty of product. I always pass up the table that looks anemic. Twenty bars of soap on a table can send mixed messages to the potential customer, the first being that you are not a serious supply for them. Poor stock may make them think, "This is just a hobby for them. If I like this soap, I bet they won't be back next month and I can't get more. I'll just try the lady a few booths down. She's here every month and has plenty." See what I mean? You never know what potential customers are thinking when they look at your table. Make sure it gives off a good first impression.

Post your soap prices on your table or in a stand up picture frame. Sometimes, customers are too shy to ask the prices, thinking they may not be able to afford them and walk away. If you have any specials such for 3-for-price or buy-three-get-one-free, post that too.

Don't forget all the little things you need when selling at a craft fair or flea market:

- cash box
- plenty of change, lots of ones
- business cards
- ink pens, notepad
- paper bags for customer purchases
- calculator

By all means, stand up when a customer approaches your table. There's nothing more unprofessional than a seller that just sits there behind their table ignoring a customer or reading a book like they could care less if you bought anything or not. Unless you have a health condition that prevents it, just sitting there sends the signal to the customer, something like this "Buy something. Don't buy something. I don't care. I can't even be bothered to get off my lazy behind and help you." Doesn't sound like a very nice sales pitch, now does it?

Most of these types of events last all day. Remember to pack lunch, several small snacks, and drinks if the venue allows you to. Some events also have food vendors. But, try not to bring a lunch with a very strong odor. The scent of your soaps usually makes the sale so don't ruin the experience with the strong whiff of onion bagels behind your table.

Just remember to be friendly and be yourself. And keep in mind that sales usually increase over time, especially if you continue to go to the same market every month - preferably in the exact same spot. Customers will begin to look for you and many times bring friends with them later on.

OTHER SALES METHODS

BED AND BREAKFASTS

Have any bed and breakfasts in your area? They usually love to offer their visitors handmade soap. To create b&b sized bars of soap, don't cut your loaf of soap into bars, not yet. First, cut the loaf in half long-ways. You now have two, long and narrow loaves of soap. Now, begin cutting these thinner loaves into thin bars. 1/2 inch thick makes a good "hotel size" bar of soap. With the two loaves you've made out of one regular sized loaf, cutting the bars 1/2 inch thick should give you about sixty bars of soap. Pricing is up to you. Charge what you feel the market will bear. Two to three times the cost of your loaf is a good starting price.

STORES AND BOUTIQUES

Pay close attention to your pricing if you are going to sell wholesale to stores and boutiques. Don't give such a huge discount that you are only making a quarter off of each bar of soap. You'll get bored and tire of that profit margin pretty quickly. If you really want to get your products into other stores be sure to ADJUST YOUR PRICES FROM THE VERY BEGINNING. In other words, don't sell your soap for $4.00 a bar at the flea market and tell the boutique on the square in town that the retail price is $7.00 a bar. Price your bars so that you can take 30 - 40% off of the retail price and still make what you feel you need to make per bar. Don't forget to include the cost of your labeling when figuring up your pricing.

BY THE SLICE

Some soap makers don't cut their batches of soap into bars at all. They keep the loaves in solid form and sell them at markets by the slice. Most often, pricing is somewhere around $1.00 - $1.50 per ounce. To sell using this method, purchase a digital scale so that you can weigh the soap right in front of the customer. You may want to pre-slice a few different sizes, weigh them and have them on display so that customers can see what an ounce, a two ounce and even a five ounce slice looks like. Over time, you'll immediately know where to cut to get pretty close to the weight the customer wants.

SELL ON YOUR WEBSITE

The title is pretty self-explanatory. But, how to set up a website is a completely different topic and a whole other story. Ask around. You can't swing a bar of soap these days without finding someone who knows how to design a website.

LABELING SOAPS

If your soap is simply soap and not considered a drug (such as acne medication soap, psoriasis soap, sunscreen soap, etc) according to the FDA, it does not require a label.

However, I've always found that I preferred to label the soaps listing the ingredients. I think customers appreciate knowing exactly what is in a bar of soap they are going to be putting on their skin. Since our soaps contain real essential oils, there is always the possibility that a customer could be allergic to a certain essential oil and they would certainly need to know it is in the recipe. One customer we have primarily buys our other body products and not our soap because she is allergic to coconut oil.

If anything, properly labeling your soaps can be very helpful in selling. Some customers are looking for certain oils or blends of oils. I've had many customers who had purchased handmade soaps from other companies in the past. When they moved or the other company went out of business, they would come to us trying to find a close replacement for their favorite bar. One lady wanted a soap with patchouli, orange and cinnamon -- that would be our holiday pomander soap. So, having the ingredients on the labels can help your customers make their selections. Anything that makes it easier for the customer can increase your sales.

Below, you will find an example of the way we like to list the ingredients on our retail soaps labels. We will use our Clove Soap as a model:

Ingredients: saponified oils of soybean, olive, coconut, and shea butter.
Essentials oils: Clove bud. *Botanicals:* powdered cloves.
Handmade and hand-cut in Tennessee

Labels also keep your company name in the customer's mind. I always tell new customers to put the labels in a drawer in their bathroom or in the linen closet. That way, when it comes time to order more soap, they don't have to try to remember what the soap was called. If YOU are new to them, they won't have to try to remember your company name, either.

Our labels have our company name first.
Then our logo.
Next, the words: handmade soap
Next, the TYPE of soap, such as CLOVE
Then, our website address
This area of the label is placed directly on the face of the soap and is part of its presentation.

By spacing down a bit on the label, I manage to include the ingredient list and have it land on the SIDE of the bar of soap.

HOW TO PACKAGE HANDMADE SOAP

Packaging handmade soaps for resale can be just as creative as the soap making process. Choices in packaging lets you express your own tastes and the look you want your company to convey to the public. There are numerous style choices - all good ones depending upon your particular market: the rustic look, boutique style, upscale salon, Victorian, simplistic or gift packaged - the possibilities are endless.

With the upsurge of the scrapbooking industry, there are countless types of beautiful papers for sale by the sheet or package. With decorative paper, you could wrap the entire bar like you would a gift, use a small strip of the decorative paper around your soap and attach together with your company label. Or, use the specialty paper like a hang tag. Get creative. Your packaging is an important marketing tool so take your time to decide how you'd like to wrap your soaps.

Plain paper, brown or even butcher style can turn out being decorative with a little effort. Wrap the bar in butcher paper just as you would a gift and tie off the bar with twine or ribbon, preferably with your company label or hangtag attached. For extra decor, get out your favorite stamps and stamp pad to liven up the paper. Even the slightest hint of color can add class to your soap packaging.

Corrugated cardboard can add wonderful texture when wrapped around a bar of soap. However, keep in mind that if your soaps are meant to be stacked for display that this method can make them a bit "wobbly". Raffia or Sisal twine tied around your bar of soap is another way to achieve that "rustic" look. Strips of muslin or even muslin tie bags are other options as well.

I usually save the more decorative effects for soap gifts sets. When it comes to our regular bars of soap, they simply have a printed cigar band around them. I do this because I want the customers to use the soap, not display it. After all, when your customers use the soap, they have to come back for more.

ON MY SOAPBOX

HAIR-PULLING TALES OF RUNNING A SOAP BUSINESS

I have to begin by telling you that I love all of our customers. I really do, even the exasperating ones. If you own a store or run a website be prepared, because these people will shop with you. It's just an extra perk you get when you own a business – funny stories and anecdotes to tell your friends and family.

One Wednesday morning, a woman was browsing through our store, picking up soaps and smelling them, oohing and aahing over her favorites. She turns to me and asks, "How do you use these?"

So, I think I didn't hear her correctly. Maybe she meant something else, like, which soaps are for certain skin problems? So, instead of pulling my hair (because I knew where this was going), I paused, took a deep breath and asked, "How do you use them? You mean, which soap is the best for dry skin?"

"No," she said. "How do you use them? What do you do with them?"

"Well, ma'am, they're bars of soap." Yes, my arms folded into the crossed position at this point.

"I know that. But what do I do with them?"

My first impression was to escort her to her car because she was clearly too dim-witted to use our products. It reminded me of that episode of *Absolutely Fabulous* when Patsy was working the sales floor in Jeremy's, a high fashion boutique. A woman comes to the door of the shop. An alarm sounds. Before the woman can enter, Patsy turns to her and says, "You can't come in. You're too fat. Get out."

"Ma'am, I don't understand the question," I said. "They are bars of soap. What are you asking me?" And the thing is, I heard her talking on her cell phone a few minutes before, holding an intelligent conversation. She was well dressed and appeared fully functional. I mean, after all, her purse and shoes matched so how mad could she be? I looked around the room. Maybe I was being Punk'd.

"Do you just get wet and use them in the shower?"

"Uh. Yeah," I said. I'm staring in disbelief at this point, wondering if she can find her way back home at night. Surely, this far into the conversation she should see how dumb her question sounded. I suddenly imagined her in the grocery store, standing next to the Charmin and stopping an employee, asking how to use the toilet paper.

"Oooh!" she says. "That's nice." She looks around the room and walks towards the door. "Thanks so much. I'll be back!"

I wave to her and can feel that my eyebrows are on top of my head. "Have a nice day!" Sometimes, you just don't know about people and what they are thinking. When you sell to the public, you have to grin, no matter what.

One of my favorite stories is the butter lady. We had accepted an invitation to sell our soaps and candles at a fundraising event. All booth rental proceeds went towards the charity; the sales of products were our own. So, Roy (my partner) and I are standing there behind our table which is loaded down with soaps, candles, lotions, and creams. In the middle of the soap sits a display of Lavender Body Butter. There's an open jar for testing and a bouquet of new popsicle sticks for dipping into the cream. A woman, about sixty years old, walks up to our booth and sniffs a few soaps. Then she smells a couple of candles. Then, she dips a giant wad of the cream onto a wooden stick and shoves it in her mouth.

I'm reaching out, trying to stop her, and my mouth is hanging open but no words would come out. The tea vendor in the booth next to us sees the whole thing happen and ducks under her table so the woman can't see her laughing.

"Uugh! What kind of butter is this?" I handed her a tissue and she began to wipe off her tongue with it. The squished-up look on her face told the whole story.

I held up the jar. "Lavender Body Butter. For the body.

The outside of the body."

"Well, you should tell people ahead of time!" She throws down the tissue and storms off, wiping her lips with the back of her sleeve.

Come on, lady, get real. You are standing in front of a booth that is filled with rows of candles and baskets of soap, all heavy with scent. The sign reads: *Soap and Candle Company*. And the first thing that occurs to you is "Yum! Something to eat!"? Oh yes; I'm sure a lot of people go into *Bath & Body Works* and drool over the brown sugar scrub and ask if it tastes good on toast. I am picturing women lined up at the Shoney's breakfast bar, rubbing pats of butter under their eyes and dabbing a little gravy behind their ears. All you can do is shake your head and smile, and then laugh when they are gone. Morons deserve good customer service too!

Then there is our bulk soap website for wholesale customers, soapbytheloaf.com. It works like this: we make the soap in full loaves or larger blocks and customers buy it at a wholesale price. They cut the soap into bars and use their own labels. No one has to ever know they didn't make the soap themselves. They don't have to learn to make soap or stock the oils in bulk, handle lye - none of that messy stuff. The customer's only task is to go to the website, click on the soaps they want, enter a credit card and wait for delivery. Sounds simple, doesn't it?

You would think so. Listen, I understand people not wanting to make soap if their business concentrates on several other products. Contrary to popular belief, it's a messy job and time consuming if it is your entire business.

But when the client is just too lazy to actually sit down and read the website - well, it just drives me up a wall. Almost daily, there are emails with questions like:

"How many bars can I get out of a loaf of soap?"
The answer is on the front page of the website.

"How much do the soap loaves weigh?"
The answer is on the front page of the website.

"Is there a minimum ordering amount?"
The answer is on the front page of the website.

There's just no way to get any actual grunt work done when you have to sit in front of the computer screen all day, replying to emails, answering questions you've already answered. About ten years ago, Oprah said that within ten years, if you could not operate a computer, it would be the same as being illiterate. It is now ten years later. Everyone she was referring to visits our wholesale site on a regular basis.

Roy and I were watching an episode of *Ace of Cakes*, the Food Network show about Charm City Cakes in Maryland. I'm paraphrasing here, but they were discussing the countless emails they receive and that most of the questions asked, were already answered on the website. I agree. Before you email a question, check - did you read the **Frequently Asked Questions** to see if the answer is already there?

So, over morning coffee, I open the email and sigh loudly. I scream a little bit. I pull my hair. Sometimes, I claw my face. Then, I politely answer the questions and provide them with the (hint-hint) link to our FAQ's page. Of course, many customers *call* to ask these same questions. I answer them calmly, most of the time while I am trying to wait on customers in the store or mixing a batch of soap. By the time they get to the third already-answered-question my temptation gets the better of me and I ask, "Have you seen our website? You're on it? Oh good. Do you know all the common questions answered on the front page? See the FAQ link? Oh good. Click on...." Aaaaah!

Now, if you think I am bashing our Soap Loaf customers, then you are incorrect. All of the above mentioned question-askers have never purchased a thing from us. It is the daydreamers that ask those questions. They entertain the thought of starting a soap business without doing a bit of research and don't seem to want to put in the work or effort that goes into it. I mean, if you can't even be bothered to read the front page of the website, you aren't going to convince me you have the passion and dedication to run a soap business. Our real customers know to point, click, buy and wait for delivery. Simple as that.

The moral of the story? If you are going to be in business and deal with the public, you are going to run into all sorts of people. Practice your smile because there are times you are going to need it.

CONCLUSION

There you have it - all the facts you need to begin this creative and addictive craft (and maybe even a business). Over the years, I've found that making soap is more than a craft; it is an art form, a creative outlet. The pride you feel when using your own soap is hard to describe. It is extremely gratifying to know that you created something out of pure, raw ingredients that will improve the health of your skin - something that will feel and smell wonderful every time you step in the shower.

A friendly warning. When you give friends and family bars of soap for testing, they will come back for more – and more after that. They are happy to be your guinea pigs, even after you have the process down pat. Eventually, they'll be asking you to put together a gift basket of your soaps for a friend's birthday. Then they want to know if you'll set up a booth at the school fair. When it all gets out of hand, do what we did - open a soap store.

Gregory White

RESOURCES & SUPPLIERS

SOAP BY THE LOAF
(wholesale bulk soap in loaves and blocks)
www.soapbytheloaf.com

BRAMBLEBERRY
(soap making supplies, ingredients)
www.brambleberry.com

MAJESTIC MOUNTAIN SAGE
(soap and bath making supplies, online lye calculator)
www.thesage.com

FROM NATURE WITH LOVE
(soap and bath making supplies)
www.fromnaturewithlove.com

AROMAWEB
(information on aromatherapy and essential oils)
www.aromaweb.com

CANDLES AND WOODCRAFTS
(wooden soap molds, displays)
www. candlesandwoodcrafts.com

SPECIALTY BOTTLE
(bottles, jars, packaging)
www.specialtybottle.com

LIBERTY NATURAL
(essential oils, aromatherapy supplies)
www.libertynatural.com

WHOLESALE SUPPLIES PLUS
(cosmetic and soap making materials)
www.wholesalesuppliesplus.com

NAHA
(National Association for Holistic Aromatherapy)
www.naha.org

INDEX

ABOUT THE AUTHOR

Gregory Lee White is a writer and a certified clinical aromatherapist. He lives in Nashville, Tennessee. His soap company is aromagregory.com author website: www.gregoryleewhite.com

Made in the USA
Middletown, DE
12 August 2016